Pope Clement

Interesting Letters of Pope Clement 14

Vol 1

Pope Clement

Interesting Letters of Pope Clement 14
Vol 1

ISBN/EAN: 9783743363878

Manufactured in Europe, USA, Canada, Australia, Japa

Cover: Foto ©Lupo / pixelio.de

Manufactured and distributed by brebook publishing software (www.brebook.com)

Pope Clement

Interesting Letters of Pope Clement 14

LETTERS

OF

POPE CLEMENT XIV.

(GANGANELLI.)

VOL. I.

INTERESTING
LETTERS

OF

POPE CLEMENT XIV.

(GANGANELLI.)

TO WHICH ARE PREFIXED,

ANECDOTES OF HIS LIFE.

TRANSLATED FROM THE FRENCH EDITION PUB-
LISHED AT PARIS BY LOTTIN LE JEUNE.

THE FIFTH EDITION.

IN TWO VOLUMES.

VOL. I.

Bique Sculp.

LONDON:
PRINTED FOR R. BALDWIN, IN PATER-NOSTER ROW; AND
T. BECKET IN THE STRAND.
M DCC LXXXI.

ANECDOTES

OF

GANGANELLI,

CLEMENT XIV.

ALTHOUGH the Chair of St. Peter is not looked upon with the same reverence in this country, at present, as it was formerly, yet the Sovereign Pontiff still holds such a rank among the Powers on the Continent, that we cannot help being astonished, to see a man of the most obscure birth, in our own days, arrive at the honour of wearing the Triple Crown; and in the mysterious ways of Providence, a petty Monk of the Order of St. Francis, which pro-

VOL. I.   B   fesses

feffes poverty, acquire fufficient power to anihilate the mighty Order of the Jefuits, thofe haughty fons of St. Ignatius, whofe cabals and intrigues had made them formidable for ages to every Court in Europe, and enabled them to eftablifh a powerful well regulated Sovereignty, in another hemifphere *.

However extraordinary it may appear, it is not the lefs true, that the fon of a Phycian, John-Vincent-Antonio Ganganelli, who was born in the year 1705, in the little town of St. Arcangelo, near Rimini, was promoted to the higheft rank of the Church, and was elected Pope, at a time when the Court of Rome was involved in the deepeft diftrefs from its quarrels with the Kings of France, Spain, Portugal, and Naples.

It has almoft always been obferved, that thofe men who have arrived at power and confequence with the world, have emited fome of thofe fparks of genius during their infancy, which anounced their future advancement; and Clement XIV. is faid

to

* Paraguay in South America.

to have given fome very fignal proofs of genius, application, and love of learning, at a very early period.

We are told that his parents were fur-prifed to fee that none of the amufements, with which other children were pleafed, could ever engage him; but they were happy to find him always with a book in his hand. He began his education at Rimini, and acquired the Latin language fo foon, that at twelve years of age he had an opportunity of addreffing a compliment to the Bifhop of Rimini in that language, who was fo ftruck with it that he foretold Ganganelli would one day be of great fer-vice to the caufe of Religion.

At the age of eighteen he left Rimini, to commence his Noviciate in the Order of St. Francis, at Urbine, at which time he took the name of *Francis-Laurence*; and very foon acquired as much credit in the Cloifter, as he had formerly done at School.

He then ftudied Philofophy and Theo-logy at Pefaro, Recanati, Fano, and Rome; and, from being a fcholar, very foon became a mafter, and taught the opinions of Scotus without being a flavifh adherent to all his dogmas.   He was much beloved by his pupils, while he taught Philofophy and Theology, at Afcoli, Bologna, and Milan; and at the age of thirty-five was called to Rome by his Superior, to teach Theology in the College of St. Bonaventura.

Though every town in Italy had fome men of genius, who owed their inftruction to Ganganelli, he wifhed to remain immured in his Cloifter; but his talents could not be concealed, and he muft have foon rifen to be General of his Order, if he had not affiduoufly prevented his Brethren from giving their voices in his favour; though, at the fame time, their implicit confidence in him was fuch, that he generally obtained their votes for whomfoever he thought the moft capable: and Father Colombini declared, that he owed the honour of being General to the recommendation of Ganganelli.

Familiar converfation, amufing books, and folitary walks, were his ufual relaxations,

ations, when he found himfelf exhaufted by intenfe ftudies. As if merit alone was not a fufficient title to the admiration of contemporaries and pofterity, fomething marvellous muft be introduced into the characters of great men; and in fuch a country as Italy, it is not furprifing that the prophecy of a Friar fhould gain credit, who is faid to have come to Ganganelli, during one of his folitary walks, and falling at his feet, to have begged his benediction, as he forefaw that he would one day be Pope; telling him, at the fame time, that he would die a violent death.

Though Ganganelli was much of a Reclufe, he was vifited in his Cell by the moft eminent for rank and learning; and fimilarity of genius recommended him to the agreeable Lambertini (Benedict XIV.) who appointed him one of the Council of the Holy Office, obferving, *that he joined an amazing memory to extenfive learning; and what is more agreeable,* added he, *he is a thoufand times more modeft than the moft ignorant, and fo chearful, that it could*

B 3

not

*not be supposed that he had ever lived in re-
tirement.*

One day, when Ganganelli was going
to Affisio, where the Founder of his Order
was born and buried, he joined a Country-
man upon the road. After an hour's
conversation, the Peasant, who had been
very attentive, said, *It is a pity that you are
only a Lay-Brother* (judging from the neg-
ligence of his dress) *for it appears to me,
that if you had studied, you might have been
another Sixtus Quintus. I have his picture
at home, and I think you have just his sly
look.*

The Italians have the story of Sixtus
Quintus so strongly imprinted upon their
minds, that even the country-people are
always talking of him, and instilling into
the minds of their children the hopes of
being Pope, because Sixtus Quintus was
elevated from the meanest condition to be
Sovereign Pontiff.

It was high time that Honours should
come in quest of Ganganelli, who had always so follicitously avoided, that a kind
of compulsion was necessary to make him

accept

accept them. The appretiators of true, merit being willing to do credit to the Sacred College, recommended him to Clement XIII. by telling him, that Ganganelli *was most humble, learned, and diligent, and that it would be doing honour to the Purple to make him Cardinal.*

The Sovereign Pontiff was easily prevailed upon. Besides its being agreeable to have worthy people recommended to him, he knew the merits of the Counsellor of the Holy Office, both from his own observation and the attention of his predecessor Benedict XIV.

· Cardinal Rezzonico, the Pope's Nephew sent immediately to the Convent of the Holy Apostles for Ganganelli, that he might announce the intentions of the Pope.

After having asked him, if he was conscious to himself that he had discharged his duty properly, and had nothing to reproach himself with, he proceeded to tell him, in a manner sufficient to intimidate him, " that a number of things had been " said of him to the Holy Father;—that

" from

" from the dread of his being too much
" affected with it, he hesitated to inform
" him of the orders of his Holiness; but
" he could not help letting him know
" that it was the Pope's pleasure, that he
" should absolutely—yes, absolutely—be
" made Cardinal."

Ganganelli was astonished at the unra-
velling of the suspence he was thrown into
by the manner of the Cardinal, who made
him imagine, at first, that somebody had
prepossessed his Holiness against him; and
falling at his feet, said, *It is no affectation of
humility, but a perfect conviction of my own
unworthiness, which engages me to declare to
you, that I by no means deserve this honour.
I protest to you, that this promotion will do no
credit to his Holiness, and will raise envy
against me, which must disturb my quiet.
If the Pope wishes to dignify our Order
with the Purple, there are more than ten
persons in our House, who, in every respect,
are more deserving of this singular favour.*

The Cardinal replied, that his Holiness,
having foreseen his unwillingness, had
positively ordered him to submit, under
pain

pain of difobedience. Ganganelli could no longer refufe, and went trembling to acquaint the Brotherhood with the news. *His Holinefs, fays he, has appointed me a Cardinal, but do not you ftartle at this new dignity. I will continue always to live with you, like one of yourfelves, always as your friend and fervant, nor fhall you ever perceive that I have changed my condition.*

It was on the 24th of Sept. 1759, that he became a Member of the Sacred College; and tho' he employed the twenty thoufand livres given yearly by the Pope to the Cardinals of the Religious Orders, to fupport the rank, yet he was neither lefs poor nor lefs modeft than he had been formerly, and kept his word with his Brotherhood moft fteadily. If he quitted his Cell, to take an apartment in the firft Dormitory, it was becaufe he was often obliged to receive vifits of ceremony. An Englifh Peer, who frequently vifited him, ufed to fay, *I cannot find the Cardinal Ganganelli; I fee only an humble Friar.*

It is faid that a General of one of the Religious Orders, having been to vifit

him,

him, left a bill upon his table for four thousand Roman crowns payable at sight; he immediately sent it after him, declaring positively, that he knew no other riches but Poverty: besides, it would lay him under obligations, and he was unwilling to contract any new engagements.

His learning and knowledge were far from being limited. He did not confine his studies to Theology and the Canon Law, but was well acquainted with the belles-lettres, politics, and sound philosophy, and even found instruction in his very amusements.

Neither the closeness of his retirement, nor the assiduity of his application, made any impression upon the natural gaiety of Ganganelli. *Every man, says he, has some wealth which is his natural inheritance, and mine is chearfulness, which is the only patrimony my parents left me, but which I value more than all the treasures of this world.*

He had a great love for foreigners, more particularly for the French, and used frequently to repeat with pleasure an incident which happened while he was a Friar at Bologna.

Bologna.   He met in his Cloifter an agreeable young petit-maitre juft come from Lyons, who faid to him, *It is only for want of fomething to do, Father, that I am walking here, for I can't endure the Monks. Perhaps, fir,* replied Ganganelli, *you may like them better in the Refectory; and if fo, I intreat you to come and take fome refrefhment.* He accepted the offer, and they entered into a converfation: with which the young man was fo pleafed, that he remained two months at Bologna, only for the pleafure of feeing Ganganelli, and by his perfuafion returned to his friends, from whom he had run away, and by whom he was tenderly beloved.   Ganganelli furnifhed him like-wife with money for his journey, and did him all the offices of a real friend.

Notwithftanding the ftrength of genius and uncommon good qualities of Ganganelli had attracted almoft univerfal ho-mage, yet there was no room to imagine that he ever would be chofen Pope.   Be-fides the freedom with which he had given his opinion with regard to fome proceedings of the Court of Rome, which did not gain

B 6   him

him the good will of the Cardinals, he had given advice fo oppofite to the fentiments of the Pontiff and his Secretary of State, on the fubject of Parma and the affair of the Jefuits, that he was no longer confulted. Clement XIII. was very well difpofed, but he had the misfortune to lofe his Secretary of State, and to choofe a fucceffor, who was too much the declared friend of the Jefuits; and this very foon produced fome difagreeable confequences. Portugal redoubled her complaints, and the affair of Parma completed the mifchief; the King of France feifed Avignon, and the King of Naples, Benevento.

Ganganelli was terrified at the ftorm which was gathering on all fides, and faw the depth of the tomb that was to bury the Roman glory, if no endeavours were ufed to calm the rage of, or if they perfifted in oppofing, the Kings.

Clement XIII. feeing himfelf preffed by the Houfes of Bourbon and Braganza, who earneftly infifted on the fuppreffion of the Jefuits, at laft appointed a meeting of the Confiftory, that he might acquaint
them

them with the neceffity of fubmitting to the
offended Kings; but the preceding night,
on the 3d of February, he unexpectedly
died. His death, which ftruck his party
with difmay, proved a confolation to the
Romans, who were chagrined at the lofs
of Avignon and Benevento, and feeing
the rage of the powerful fovereigns ready
to burft upon their heads, had no hopes but
in a new reign. The death of every Pope
occafions matter both of joy and forrow.

The meeting of the Conclave in fuch a
critical fituation, was like a cloudy fky,
or rather a tempeft. The Cardinals met;
almoft all of them, however, were of different opinions. Some were for choofing a
Pontiff, who would ftruggle againft the
power of the Kings; while others were
equally defirous of electing one who would
prove agreeable to them: both parties dif-
puted with great zeal.

The choice of a Pope is always a work
of labour, on account of the number of
voices neceffary to determine the Election.
The Sacred College is commonly compofed of three parties; the Pious, the Politic,
and

the Indifferent. The firſt contend obſti-
nately for electing him whom they believe to be the moſt deſerving; the ſe-
cond are determined by their intereſts,
or the influence of the crowned heads;
while the third are blown about by every
wind; which gave riſe to the true ſaying,
That he who goes Pope *into the Conclave,
generally comes out a* Cardinal.

Ganganelli was unconnected with any
party, and almoſt ſingle, when he was
aſked by ſome of the Cardinals if he choſe
to be Pope: *As you are too few to nominate
me,* anſwered he, *and too many to keep my
ſecret, you ſhall know nothing.*

The Emperor was at this time in Rome,
and viſited the Conclave, but did not
ſpeak a word in favour of Ganganelli, nor
even ſuſpect that he would be elected.
Aſtoniſhed only at ſeeing him in a black
habit, he took him for a Friar; when
Ganganelli in a low voice ſaid, *He is a
Religious of the Order of St. Francis, and
wears the livery of poverty.*

Paſquinades, which have always been
in uſe at Rome, and more particularly
during

during the fittings of the Conclave, were
at this time multiplied on all fides. As
they generally declare the prevailing opinions, it may not be amifs to take notice
of fome which characterifed Ganganelli.
One in Latin applied to himfelf thefe words
of the 118th Pfalm, *Super docentis me intel-
lexi*; " I know more than my inftructors."
Another in Italian reprefented him as
having teeth to bite, and a good nofe to
fmell:

A denti per moficare,
E buon azo per fentire

Thefe were the more favourable, as
lampoons at thofe times fpare nobody.
Some of the Cardinals were reprefented
as not being able to fpeak —*Ab nefcio loqui;*
and others as only having a human form—
Animal quafi habens faciem hominis, &c.
&c. &c.

The Conclave lafted three months and
fome days, and became tumultuous from
the difficulties which occurred in nomina-
ting a Pontiff. The Jefuits had a number

of

of Cardinals who were attached to them, and dreaded the fubmiffion of their Order; while their opinions were counterbalanced by others, who found means to unite the caufe of Politics with Religion, to fupport the rights of the Holy See, and yield at the fame time to the requifitions of the Sovereign Princes.

The Cardinals, attached to the Houfe of Bourbon, knew, that though Ganganelli had no hatred againft the Jefuits, he never cultivated their friendfhip; that while Profeffor of Theology, he had frequently combated their opinions, and explained himfelf openly, upon the neceffity of coming to an agreement with the Kings; and that he thought, whenever any Religious Order became obnoxious to the Catholic Powers, it ought to be fuppreffed.

Befides this, there was a Friar with whom he had frequently correfponded upon the tranfactions of Clement XIII. who thought that it was for the intereft of the Church to acquaint the French Minifter with this correfpondence. His manner of thinking, therefore, being found totally

totally different from the late fyftem, and it appearing extremely probable that he would fecond the views of the Houfe of Bourbon, Louis XV. gave pofitive orders to Cardinal de Bernis to fupport the election of Ganganelli. De Bernis, a man of great abilities, having drawn off Cardinal Rezzonico and his party to the fide of France and Spain, gained an important victory, inafmuch as it decided the election in favour of Ganganelli, and feated in the Chair of St. Peter the man who was moft worthy to fill it. Thus of old did the eloquence of Aaron frequently ferve to accomplifh the defigns of God.

We may judge from this fimple narrative of facts, whether there could be any foundation for the contemptible fatires which faid that Clement XIV. obtained the Triple Crown, on condition that he would fupprefs the order of Jefuits. Ganganelli defpifed honours too much, and his confcience was too delicate, to fubmit to fuch conditions. But the fate of the greateft men is to have two characters: while they are extolled by fome, they are defamed by others.

On

On the 19th May, 1769, the Sacred College, finding that Ganganelli would be agreeable to the Kings, and knowing him to be both learned and virtuous, proclaimed him Sovereign Pontiff. He was then seen to appear like a rainbow in the Heavens, iffuing from a thick cloud to announce the return of fine weather. He was defirous to have taken the name of Sixtus VI. but in gratitude to Clement XIII. who had made him Cardinal, he took the name of Clement, according to an old eftablifhed cuftom.

He was fo little dazzled with his promotion, that next morning he could fcarcely be awaked; for, moft unlike an ambitious man, he had never flept more found. When the ceremony of Adoration was over, he was afked, if he was tired? and replied in his ufual, humble, natural manner, *That he had never feen that ceremony more at his eafe; particularly as he recollected how he had been fqueezed on a fimilar occafion, when he was only a fimple Friar.*

It is incredible how the people rejoiced, when they were informed of his being chofen.

Nothing

Nothing but ſhouts of joy were heard: and, as a Venetian Lady wrote to her friends, "the world was tranſported with "joy, as if the Golden Age was to re- "turn." But, alas! it was only the dawn of a fine day, which was to end with the morning.

He was deſired to ſend a Courier to in- form his ſiſters of his promotion; but he was content to write by the poſt, ſaying, *they were not uſed to receive ambaſſadors.*

No Pope was ever elected in more tem- peſtuous times. Portugal was about to chooſe a Patriarch, and lay aſide all com- munication with the Pope; and the Kings of France, Spain, and Naples, threat- ened to take ſome ſteps fatal to the Court of Rome. Venice propoſed to reform their religious Communities, without paying any attention to the Holy See. Poland wanted to diminiſh the privileges of the Nuncio, and to check the Papal power; while the Romans themſelves murmured at ſeeing their poſſeſſions fall into the hands of ſtrangers. And to complete all theſe misfortunes, a madneſs was ſpreading far and

and wide, which attacked Kings and Pontiffs, and even God himself, by ranking Christianity in the same class with superstitious chimeras. What a prospect for the Head of the Church!

Clement XIV. began to reign by addressing vows to Heaven for the necessities of the church and State; and, in the next place, by writing to the different Monarchs, to show his pacifick disposition. He appointed Cardinal Palavicini to be his Secretary of State, as a Minister agreable to the kings; but with an intention to govern by himself, and to preserve his intentions in inviolable secrecy from the whole world.

The affair of the Jesuits was urged daily by the different Princes and their Ambassadors; but such was the moderate spirit of Ganganelli, whose love of justice made him weigh every grievance with the minutest attention before he would decide, that four years were employed in the examination.

Like an indulgent parent, he took the first steps to lead to an accommodation with Portugal, and succeeded in re-establishing

the

the ancient friendſhip which had ſubſiſted between the two Courts.

He was crowned in St. Peter's the 4th of June 1769, amidſt the loudeſt acclamations; and on the 26th of November following, he took poſſeſſion of St. John de Lateran, with all the magnificence which uſually accompanies that pompous ceremony.

His love of peace, and his follicitude to accommodate matters with the offended Kings, made him omit ſome ceremonies at a time when they were expected with their uſual eclat; and as this was the effect of his own authority, without any previous conſultation, the Cardinals concluded that he was not to be led, nor even his intentions to be divined.

Though he was happy in his native ſimplicity of manners, Ganganelli knew when to aſſume the magnificence of a ſovereign Pontiff, and how to diſplay the auguſt character with the greateſt dignity; as was ſeen when the Duke of Glouceſter viſited Rome. Indeed ſtrangers of every country and every rank met with the moſt engaging

reception

reception, and were all anxious to fee a difciple of St. Francis who had been preferred to the Roman Princes, and the fons of Kings, in an age moſt unfavourable to his profeſſion.

That he might neither be betrayed, nor have his intentions difcovered, he treated with the Kings himfelf; and by his attention to the wants of the people, guarded againſt the evils by which the Ecclefiaſtical State had been diſtreffed in the time of his predeceſſor, from the villainy of monopolifers, who had . fent the provifions to Venice which ſhould have fupplied the Romans.

The Cardinals murmured at his want of confidence; but he faid, *That a Sovereign, who had a number of confidents, was infallibly governed, and often betrayed;—I ſleep found when my fecret is my own.*

His manner of living, was as abſtemious, when he was Pope, as it had been while he was Friar at the Convent of the Holy Apoſtles. When he was told that Papal Dignity required a more fumptuous table, he anfwered, *That neither St. Peter nor St.*

Francis

Francis had taught him to dine splendidly; and whe n the head-cook of the Kitchen came to beg that he might be continued; he said to him, *You shall not lose your appointment, but I will not lose my health to keep your hand in.*

He was reproached with being too indulgent in granting Briefs of Secularization; but he considered a discontented Monk as a perpetual disgrace to the community. The greatest satisfaction he derived from his being appointed Cardinal, was the power of sometimes assisting his neighbour; and he never went abroad without giving some instances of his liberality, which were always accompanied with the most pleasing language.

A proof of his having the resolution, if he had not the severity of Sixtus Quintus, was his arresting the Marquis of——for having given the Count of —— a box on the ear in publick, and sending him instantly to the Castle of St. Angelo, to remain there for seven years. Yet no man shewed greater sensibility than he did when he

was

informed of a criminal being fentenced to die.

He difcouraged every kind of flattery, and no man was eafier with his friends. He would difpute with the learned, talk politics with the ftatefman, converfe with foreigners, and be fociable with his bre-thren of St. Francis.   One evening he faid *I have been a Prince and a Pope all day. That I may not be quite fuffocated, I muft be Father Ganganelli again.—Come, let us chat as we ufed to do.*

To the little artifices practifed by nar-row minds to obtain their ends, he was a ftranger.   Though peculiarly calculated for a Court, which is accufed of being the very vortex of intrigue and chicane, he never deceived the Politicians, but by remaining filent; for when he fpoke he uttered the truth.   He was too upright a man to act by finifter means, and had, in-deed, too great a genius to ftand in need of them.

No one knew better when to feize the proper moment, when he was neither flow nor precipitate. " The hour is not come," he he would fay, when he was follicited to haften fome operation. He wrote to Cardinal Stoppani, " I miftruft my vivacity, " and therefore I fhall not anfwer till the " end of a week, concerning what your " Eminency requires of me. Our imagi- " nation is often our greateft enemy; I " am ftriving to weary mine before I act. " Bufinefs, like fruit, hath its time of " maturity, and we fhould never think " of difpatching it, when it is only half " ripe."

His manner of reading refembled his other operations; he abftained from books, if he found himfelf difpofed to reflect; and as Sovereigns are led by circumftances, from whence we may couclude that all men are born dependent, he often kept vigils great part of the night, and flept in the day-time. " Their Rule, he ufed to " fay, is the compafs of Monks and Friars; " but the wants of their people is the clock " of fovereigns: be it what hour it may, " if they want us we muft attend them."

La buſſola di frati è la lora regola, ma il biſogno del popolo è l'orologio dei ſovrani.

This

This maxim, when he was Pope, often interrupted his ftudies. He then read only to edify himfelf, or to relax from bufinefs. He was of opinion, that all the books in the world might be reduced to fix thoufand volumes in folio, and that thofe of the prefent age were nothing but paintings, which daubers had found the art of cleaning and varnifhing, in order to prefent them in a new or frefher light to the publick view.

It is to be lamented that he produced nothing in the literal way, though fome have afcribed to him part of the works of Benedict XIV. We fhould have found in his writings the phlegm of the Germans, blended with the vivacity of the Italians; but he was fo thoroughly perfuaded that there were too many Writers, that he was always fearful of increafing the number. He faid one day, fmiling, " Who knows " whether Brother Francis may not one " day take it into his head to write? I " fhould not be in the leaft aftonifhed to " fee fome Work in his manner; but " furely it will not be an hiftory of my " ragouts,

" ragouts, or the book muſt be very conciſe!"

When any one mentioned to him the faſhionable productions that appeared againſt Chriſtianity, he would ſay, " The " more there are, the more the world " will be convinced of the neceſſity of it." He obſerved, " That all the Writers who " oppoſed Chriſtianity, knew only how to " dig a ditch, without having any thing " to ſupply its place with." He ſaid, " That M. Voltaire, whoſe poetry he ad- " mired, attacked Religion ſo often, only " becauſe it was troubleſome to him;" " and that J. J. Rouſſeau was a painter, " who always failed in the heads, and ex- " celled only in the drapery."

He explained himſelf one day upon a Work called *The Syſtem of Nature,* and added, " What hurts me is, that the " more it is founded upon falſe principles, " the more, in an age like our's, it will " gain reputation and readers; and it will " receive an additional value by its being " ſeriouſly refuted." He afterwards ob- ſerved, " that the Author of this bad " Book is a madman, who imagines,

C 2   " that

" that by changing the master of the house,
" he can dispose of it just as he pleases,
" without reflecting, that no creatures
" can breath but by existing in God: *In*
" *ipso vivimus, movemur, & sumus.*

" But every age is distinguished by a
" new mode of thinking. After the times
" of superstition are come the days of
" infidelity; and a man who formerly a-
" dored a multitude of gods, now affects
" not to acknowledge any one. Virtue,
" vice, immortality, annihilation, all ap-
" pear to him synonimous terms, while some
" slight Pamphlet serves him as a rampart
" against Heaven; and it is in the very
" bosom of Religion that these scandalous
" opinions originate and multiply. Whilst
" Religion was persecuted by the Pagans,
" a Pope had at least the glory and
" the good fortune to defend it at the
" price of his blood; but now that he
" cannot bear testimony to the faith by
" martyrdom, he is unfortunately com-
" pelled to be the sorrowful witness of
" error and impiety."

These

These excellent reflections he made in the presence of a Commander of Malta, from whom the Author had them, and who assured him that the Pope was ever ready to sacrifice himself for the good of Religion, and the interests of the Church, considering his life as no object when these were called in question.

It was solely for the glory of the Church that he from time to time created several Cardinals, without the least regard to his own personal interests, or connexions of affinity.

Their institution, which commences in the ninth century, had no other object than the benefit and honour of Religion. They constitute the Council of the Sovereign Pontiffs, when they have occasion for advice; and there were at all times amongst them persons of eminence, whose zeal, added to their knowledge, proved of infinite use to the church and State. Some carried their courage and their faith to the extremities of the world; others, with the approbation of Princes, governed with wisdom the most flourishing Empires.

C 3   The

The lateſt poſterity will remember with admiration, the Amboiſes, Ximenes, Richelieus, and Fleurys, and conſider them as the bulwarks of thoſe kingdoms where they acted as Miniſters.

If Clement XIV. did not make any complete promotion of Cardinals during his Pontificate, it is to be ſuppoſed that he was reſtrained by other Powers, or that he was embarraſſed in the ſelection of proper objects. He might probably rather chooſe to come to no determination, than to difpleaſe any of his old friends, who flattered themſelves with the hopes of obtaining the Purple, and neverthelefs might not be worthy of it. The good qualities necefſary in friendſhips are not ſufficient for a Cardinal. It is a dignity that has too much influence upon the Church, to be conferred indiſcriminately.

To judge properly of the genius of Clement, we ſhould view him with ſome friends, and particularly the Cardinal de Bernis (whoſe different periods of life ſeem to have been diſtinguiſhed by the moſt flattering epochas, and the moſt deli

cate

cate works of genius) conferring upon
the fubjects of the times, and the means of
reconciling the interefts of Religion with
thofe of the Princes. When the greateft
lights had been thrown by thefe his Coun-
fellors upon the fubject in debate, Ganganelli, as the *primum mobile* of their deli-
berations, decided with manly refolution.
The flighteft error would have been of the
moft dangerous confequence. The chief
point in queftion was to weigh the rights of
the Sovereign Pontiff with the motives which
fhould rule his actions, and to keep within the bounds that fupport the equilibrium
between the Holy Father and the other
Potentates.

The more arduous and difficult are the
functions of a Pope, the more he ftands in
need of repofe to enable him to fuftain his
labours. Caftel-Gandolfo, built by the
Chevalier Bernini, four leagues from
Rome, near the Lake Albano, which commands the moft agreeable profpects, is the
ufual fummer refidence of the Sovereign
Pontiffs.

Clement

Clement failed not to repair thither in the months of May and October, the most proper feafons in Italy to enjoy the pleafures of the country; and it was here, to be intimately acquainted with him, we should view him anatomizing an infect, analyzing a flower, purfuing the phænomena of nature, by degrees rifing up to her Author, and at length taking a general view of Earth and Heaven; or retiring within himfelf in private meditation; or, at other times familiarly converfing with his friends and intimates.

His imagination was raifed at the fight of thofe beauties that prefent themfelves in the neighbourhood of Rome to the recollection of the ancient Romans, who had fo boldly trampled upon the foil: he recalled to his memory the moft fublime and ingenious paffages of the ancient Poets upon the occafion. There are few Italians of any education, who are unacquainted with the Works of Ariofto, Dante, Taffo, Petrach, and Metaftafio; even the women amufe themfelves with the perufal of

thefe

thefe Poets, and can quote them occa-fionally.

His Philofophy ferved his imagination as an excellent fecond; it recalled to his memory the different fituations of his life; at one time in a ftate of obfcure tranquil-lity, then forcibly agitated in the glare of dignity: like a pilot, who, after a calm fe-rene morning, in the evening finds himfelf in a violent hurricane, accompanied with thunder, hail, and rain.

Sometimes, weary of meditation, he would retire with an old Convent Friend, Brother Francis, into fome private arbour where they could not be feen. There fome Cloyfter anecdotes amufed them, and they feemed in a perfect ftate of equality. One day, Clement pointing to him, re-peated thefe words: " He has kept his " habit, and is happier than I am, who " wear the Tiara. It was decreed I fhould " be a Pope, and I very much fear (here " he paufed)—however, we muft fubmit " to the will of God."

He was once entertaining himfelf in this manner, when fome Ambaffadors

were anounced to him. They found him
as ferene and compofed as if nothing had
agitated his mind; but he could not help
fmiling fometimes at the perplexities his
manners and conduct muft have occafioned
in the curious.

While he was at Caftel-Gandolfo, on
giving a fplendid repaft to fome Grandees
of Spain, he laid afide his Sovereign authority, and joined them in a friendly manner
when feated at table, without fuffering
them to rife to falute him.

The public imagined he had loft fight of
the grand affair of the Jefuits, whilft according to the cuftom of the Court of Rome
he only fought to gain time. He fometimes fearched the archives of the *Propa-
ganda*, to confult the Memoirs of Cardinal
de Tournon, of M. Maigrot, of La
Beaumé, and of the Jefuit Miffionaries.
At other times he had read to him the ac-
cufations brought againft the Society, and
their vindications. Every important publication, *pro* or *con*, refpecting the Jefuits,
he attentively examined; whilft equally
diftrufting the eulogiums and the farcafms
                                        paffed

paffed upon them, he was biaffed neither by their Panegyrifts nor their Satirifts. No man was ever more impartial. Equally abftracting himfelf from his own inclinations as well as all prejudices, he judged in the fame manner upon the occafion, as pofterity neceffarily muft. "Let me "(faid he to the Sovereigns who preffed "him to determine) have leifure to exa- "mine the important bufinefs upon which "I am to pronounce. I am the common "Father of the Faithful, particularly of "the Religious; and I cannot deftroy "a celebrated Order without having fuf- "ficient reafons to juftify me in the "eyes of all ages, and above all before "God."

The people, ever idolizing him, ceafed not to blefs his reign; and their perfeverance in doing fo conftitutes his greateft eulogium. It is well known that the Romans eafily change from enthufiafm to hatred; that they have often calumniated thofe Pontiffs whom they have flattered the moft; and that a Pope to pleafe them, fhould not reign above three years. Un-

C 6   happy

happy on account of their lazinefs, they conftantly hope, that a change of mafters muft be attended with an increafe of happinefs! juft as fick men are apt to fancy that they fhall be much eafier when they are placed in another pofture.

The glory of Clement would not have been complete, if he had not contributed to the embellifhment of Rome, a city fo fufceptible of ornaments, and fo fertile in riches proper to decorate it. Willing, therefore, to purfue the paths of Sixtus V. Paul V. and Benedict XIV. he compofed a Mufeum, comprizing every thing that could gratify the curiofity of Antiquaries and Travellers; that is to fay, of the fcarceft curiofities that have been tranfmitted by the Ancients.

It might be faid, on this occafion, that Rome, defirous of honouring his Pontificate, was eager to difplay the mafterpieces of art which lay concealed within her bowels. Scarce a year paffed without vafes, urns, or ftatues of exquifite workmanfhip being dug up, to enrich the fuperb collection begun under Lambertini.

Here,

Here, with the glance of an eye, we may see the triumph of the Chriſtian Religion, by the fragments that were uſed in the Pagan ſacrifices, and the ruins of all thoſe prophane Divinities, whoſe ſtatues are no longer held in eſtimation, but in proportion to the maſterly manner with which they are executed.

When Clement could relax from the variety of buſineſs in which he was engaged, he viſited theſe monuments with Foreigners of diſtinction, and celebrated Artiſts, rather as a Sovereign who conſiders it as a duty to embelliſh his capital, than as an *Amateur* who gratifies his taſte.   This he ſaid to the Chevalier Chatelus, a worthy deſcendent of the immortal D'Agueſſeau, as well on account of his wit as his extenſive knowledge.   After converſing with him upon different ſubjects, he added, "that being born in a Village, and "brought up in a Cloyſter, where the love "of the arts was not inſpired, he could "not acquire the neceſſary judgement to "determine as a Connoiſſeur upon the "monuments he had collected; but that, as a "Sovereign;

" Sovereign, he thought himself obliged
" to difplay the fineft models to the eyes
" of Artifts and the Curious, that they
" might know and imitate them."

If he did not always reward the Learned
as they might think they had a right to
expect from fo enlightened a Pope, circumftances fhould be adverted to. The
multiplicity of bufinefs in which he was
engaged, joined to the fhortnefs of his
reign, did not afford him leifure to engage in thofe purfuits which would have
given him the greateft pleafure. Moreover, a Pope cannot always act agreeably
to his own inclinations. There are incidents that tie up his hands. Neverthelefs,
he was always found attentive to beftow
Bifhoprics upon thofe only whom he knew
to be men of learning; and to this reafon
may be afcribed his fo frequently promot-
ing priefts of his own Order.

A Pope is generally very circumfpect in
the nomination of a Bifhop. He knows
that the proper government of a diocefe
requires judgement and abilities; for
which reafon the Italian Bifhops are ufually

as

as humble as they are learned, and as charitable as they are zealous. They are conſtant reſidents, and live in friendſhip and cordiality with their Curates; for they muſt not be confounded with thoſe *Monſig-nori* known in Rome under the titles of *Prelati*, and who frequently, not being even in Orders, fill ſuch poſts as Laymen might occupy, and ſerve the Pope in his various functions.

Clement was not leſs attentive in the nomination of his Nuncios: he was de-ſirous that his Ambaſſadors ſhould do him honour, as well by their manners as by their learning, and particularly by their love of peace. And if he appointed M. Doria his Nunico to the Court of France, not-withſtanding his youth, it was becauſe he was convinced that his extraordinary vir-tues had outſtripped his years, and that his merit had already correſponded with the celebrity of his name. It was not till after the conſequence this Prelate had gained in Spain (where he was the bearer of the conſecrated child-bed linen) that Clement named him Nuncio in France.

He

He sent him there as an Angel of Peace, capable of maintaining the harmony between the Father and the eldest Son of the Church.

Religion has often suffered by an indiscrete zeal; and in order to prevent it for the future, as far as possible, Clement, whose prudence ever dictated all his motions and resolves, observed the Evangelical toleration which the Divine Legislator made use of towards the Sadducees and the Samaritans. He used to say, " We " too often lay aside Charity to maintain " Faith; without reflecting, that if it is " not allowed to tolerate error, it is for-" bidden to hate and persecute those who " have unfortunately embraced it."

He watched attentively over the Pontifical treasures. Besides paying all the expences of the Conclave when he was chosen, some debts of the Apostolical Chamber, and all those of his predecessor; he established some manufactures, and amply provided for the expences of the state, while he gave pensions to decayed gentlemen and new converts.

The

The œconomy of Ganganelli made the treafures of the ftate fufficiently fupport the publick expences, and do many acts of liberality, befides fupplying a confiderable expence in receiving the Princefs Dowager of Saxe, and the Brothers of the King of England, whom he entertained moft royally.

But what redounds more to his credit, and is very fingular in the hiftory of a Pope, he never once thought of raifing his own family at the publick charge, but, on the contrary, feemed totally to neglect them; although it had been the practice of his predeceffors to raife their Nephews to the higheft honours.

The hiftory of Nepotifm, which has been the rock upon which all the popes have fplit, informs us, that the moft devout among them, enriched their Nephews the moft, and raifed them to the greateft honours.

No man ever fet a more ftriking example of difintereftednefs. He even declined to accept of a fine fnuff box; and pulling out his old one from his fleeve,

faid

said it had been his companion in his cell for forty years, and he never would have another.

Rome had long suffered from Quacks, who practised without interruption; but Clement XIV. soon put a stop to the practice of all who were not regularly approved.

An instance where he showed unusual vigour, was upon hearing that one *Peter Andrea* had fraudulently exported some grain to Finmicino, in the Pope's own gallies. Forgetting his natural mildness of temper, and seeing only the danger to which his people might be exposed by such villainy, he could not contain himself. *Send him to prison,* said he, *and let him be immediately tried, that the publick may know, that it is death to me to see the substance of my subjects diminished.*

After the strictest examination of every argument that could be produced either against or in favour of the Jesuits, during an enquiry which continued four years, Clement XIV. at last named a Commission, consisting of five Cardinals, some Prelates,

lates, and Advocates, to affist him in the execution of his defign; and after the matureft deliberation, figned the Brief on the 21ft of July, 1773, which fuppreffed that famous Order. On the 10th of Auguft following, at nine o'clock in the evening, the Commiffioners appointed for the execution of the Brief, accompanied by a Notary, and attended by a guard, went to the different Houfes of the Jefuits; and having affembled the Brethren, read to them the Brief of their extinction; at the fame time telling them, that the Apoftolical Chamber would furnifh each of them with a fecular habit, pay the travelling expences of thofe who chofe to quit Rome—that their books and effects fhould be delivered to them—and that they fhould have penfions.

As the Jefuits had a great fhare in the education of youth, the fhutting up their fchools might have proved of bad confequence, if Clement had not given a new proof of his attention, genius, and abilities. Having fhut himfelf up for fome days, and fketched out a plan of education

worthy

worthy of the greateſt maſter; he caſt a rapid eye upon ſome Prieſts and Friars who by their talents and example were capable of replacing the Jeſuit teachers, and immediately inſtituted them Profeſſors: ſo that, to the aſtoniſhment of Rome, there ſeemed to be ſcarce any interval between the departure of the Jeſuits and the coming of their Succeſſors; the ſchools being again opened at the very inſtant when the Public thought they muſt have remained ſhut up for a long time.

The ſuppreſſion of the Jeſuits having taken place, the Kings and the Venetian ſtate immediately accommodated the diſputes which had ſubſiſted ſo long between them and the Court of Rome.

Clement naturally poſſeſſing a robuſt conſtitution, the regularity in which he lived promiſed a long life; but the multiplicity of intricate affairs in which he was involved, agitated his mind ſo much, that his health could not fail to be affected. In the month of April 1775, he was firſt obſerved to decline, and ſoon after was tormented with cruel pains in his bowels,

bowels, with which he languished for five months, without the Phyficians being able to difcover the caufe of his diforder, or to afford him the leaft relief. Upon his death, which happened on the 22d of September, his body turned inftantly black, and appeared in a ftate of putrefaction, which induced the people prefent to impute his death to the effect of Poifon; and it was very generally reported that he had fallen a facrifice to the refentment of the Jefuits.

Thus died Francis-Laurens Ganganelli, aged 69 years, 10 months, and 22 days, after having arrived at the higheft dignity in the moft turbulent times, without having been for one fingle inftant dazzled by his elevation, or difmayed by the troubles he had to encounter. His life was a model for future Popes; and his death a leffon to all good Chriftians.

He was of an ordinary ftature, had a large forehead, black and very thick eyebrows, lively eyes, and a long vifage.

P R E-

PREFACE

BY M. CARACCIOLI.

THE aſtoniſhing ſale of theſe Letters ſufficiently proclaims their merit. Their authenticity cannot be doubted, if we would judge of them merely from their ſtriking conformity with the knowledge, genius, and conduct of Clement XIV.

Beſides the honourable teſtimonies which Foreigners and the Learned in every part of Europe had rendered to Ganganelli, before he was advanced to the Papal Chair, as to a perſon of the greateſt affability and impartiality, with the moſt enlightened underſtanding, and moſt pacifick turn of mind; the ſuppreſſion of the Bull *In Cœna Domini*, and the perfect harmony which he re-eſtabliſhed between the Court of Rome

and

and the offended Kings, muſt ſhow the world that this immortal Pontiff was not led by opinions or prejudices, but that he really thought too much reſpect could not be paid to Sovereigns who had been on all occaſions the protectors of the Holy See, and that the Popes can never be more powerful than when ſupported by the Houſe of Bourbon.

The Letters of Clement XIV. are fully authenticated by his conduct and by his ſentiments. They diſplay the ſame religious principles which he always taught in publick; the ſame maxims which he obſerved in his life; and the ſame underſtanding which made him keep at a diſtance whatever favoured either of fanaticiſm or ſuperſtition.

But what more evidently proves that theſe Letters are not counterfeit—I had copied a number of them in the year 1758, at Florence, from the originals which were communicated to me by the Prelate Cerati, and the Abbé Lami, and was deſirous to publiſh them in the year 1762, when I received the following anſwer from P. Ganganelli

ganelli (then Cardinal), whofe consent I wished to obtain; an answer which at present lies before me, and which I can show to any one who is desirous of seeing it.

SIR,

THE Letters which have been communicated to you at Florence were written in haste, and by no means deserve the honour you are inclined to confer on them, by a publication; I most earnestly beg of you, therefore, not to give them to the public. What I have written can have no other merit, than candour and truth. I am not the less obliged to you, and shall always acknowledge the affection you have shown for me. I shall seek every opportunity of testifying my gratitude, and proving to you with what esteem I declare myself

Your sincere humble Servant,

F. LAUR. CARD. GANGANELLI.
ROME, 19 Sept. 1762.

It is evident, then, that from the year 1762, I had been in possession of genuine Letters of P. Ganganelli; and it is not less evident, that those which have come to my

VOL. I.   D   hands,

hands, in the courfe of the laft year, have fuch a refemblance to thefe, that they cannot be miftaken. The author of the *Journal des Sciences & des Beaux Arts* fays, with reafon, " That if they will only ac-" knowledge three of the Letters to be " thofe of Clement XIV. it is neceffary " that they fhould all be fo; for the fame " foul and the fame genius feem to have " dictated the whole."

Connoiffeurs are not to be deceived, and with only a little tafte and practice, copies are to be diftinguifhed from origi-nals, as eafily in Letters as in Painting. The foul of Clement XIV. is feen through-out the whole, and That cannot be co-pied. Befides, what is there extraordi-nary in all this?—That Ganganelli, who having attained to be a Cardinal, and af-terwards to be a Pope, by his merit; who was declared in a full Confiftory, by the famous Father Berti, in a publick Act, to be a Perfon of whom Rome fhould be proud; who was boafted of as a moft ele-gant Panegyrift by a number of towns in Italy; marked out by the great Lam-

bertini

bertini (Benedict XIV.) as a subject of the higheft hopes; in fhort cited as a man of moft rare accomplifhments, by every Writer in Italy: what is there, I fay, extraordinary, in his having written ingenious and learned Letters? If the fpirit of Party-had not wifhed to pafs Ganganelli upon the world for a man of middling parts, this matter could never have been brought into queftion.

If Clement XIV. had left a powerful family; if a fpirit of Party had been difcernible in thefe Letters; or, if the mediocrity of the Work had required a refpectable name to impofe upon the Publick, paffion or intereft might have been fufpected: but in the prefent cafe, the genuinenefs of this felection is irrefutable.

It is an act of the greateft injuftice to accufe the Italians of knowing nothing but fuperftitious devotion. The moft excellent book of enlightened piety which is now extant amongft the Catholicks, was written by Muratori; and no perfon of that Communion can be ignorant of Benedict XIV. having proved, both by his dif-

courfes

courfes and writings, the fovereign contempt in which he held every thing that
marked only a trifling attention to mere
church ceremonies: nor is it a fecret to the
Learned World, that the Sacred College
has always abounded with men of the
brighteft parts.

It is no lefs certain, that amongft the
Religious in Cloifters, efpecially in Italy,
many individuals may be found, who have
knowledge, principles, and extenfive views,
yet want opportunities of difplaying their
talents fufficiently to become great men.
For example, place P. Gerdil, a religious
Barnabite, and Preceptor to the Prince of
Piedmont, in a confpicuous light, and you
will then behold genius and learning fhine
forth, with a piety totally free from Pharifaical zeal, and Party fpirit. Though
Rome is no longer deemed the Miftrefs of
the World, either in arms or arts, yet to
difpute the ability of the Italians to write
fenfible, ingenious Letters, is to betray
an extreme ignorance of their national
charaƈteriftick.

The

The objection made to thefe Letters, " That there are people at Rome who " know nothing of them," does not deferve to be refuted. We do not call in friends or neighbours to ferve as witneffes, when we fit down to write; and it frequently happens, that even thofe with whom we live in the greateft intimacy, may not be acquainted with the abfent friends with whom we correfpond *.

" It would give this work (fay its op-" ponents) a greater appearance of origi-" nality and candour, if we were to men-" tion the fource from whence we had ob-" tained thefe Letters. " But as this is a matter of confidence, and that the perfons from whom we receive them are unwilling to appear, we are by no means intitled to break the feal of fecrecy, under which they were entrufted to our hands. It requires no great exertion of genius to divine the motives of their caution; perhaps they may one day declare them, and it will be

D 3 feen

---

* See Letter CXVII. firft paragraph, where Ganganelli vouches this very article himfelf.

feen that their prefent referve was juftly founded.

The inaccuracy of the dates, which are correćted in this Edition, had no other origin but in the great hurry of the Printers: the greater thefe faults, the lefs ought they to be afcribed to the Editor.

The great number of Italian words found in the firft Edition, having difpleafed many people of tafte, by their breaking the difcourfe, or introducing a medley which was not in the original Letters, I have retrenched almoft all the citations, or, rather, have tranflated them into the text.

I have retouched the Letters to Louis XV. Madame Louifa, the Duke of Parma, &c. when it will be feen (as far as the ftile of the Roman Chancery could admit of it) that they truely refemble the other Letters. I have likewife reviewed the Italian, and have found fome faults in the tranflation, which will not appear now, as the thoughts are given in their proper fenfe. It appeared to me, that as all the three Warrants addreffed to Monfignor Giraul, his Holinefs

nefs's Nuncio, on the fubject of Madame Louifa's profeffion and taking the habit, expreffed the fame thing, one would be fufficient.

If the *Supplement*, which the Publick have impatiently expected, has not appeared, it is becaufe the Works of Ganganelli are not fabricated in France, as has been reported; and that authentick Pieces are ftill wanting to complete it. Thofe which I have already, with fome that are promifed, will enable me to give another Volume, quite diftinct from, but not lefs interefting than, the Letters; where fome curious anecdotes and pieces of fingular eloquence will be met with. M. L'Abbé Fabri, Nephew of Clement XIV. will undertake to publifh the Theological Treatifes compofed by his Uncle, which are in the higheft efteem.—In his Letter to me from Rome, of the 6th of February laft, he fays, *Li quali di qui a non molto in fteffo mandero alla luce.*

Nothing more remains to be faid, than that Pofthumous Works are almoft always fufpected; and though a decree of Parlia-

D 4 ment

ment was obtained formerly, by Monf. Boffuet, Bifhop of Troyes, affirming to the Publick, that certain productions which he publifhed under the name of his Uncle the Bifhop of Meaux, were truely the works of that great Prelate; yet there are many people who will not believe it. It is to be obferved, however, that it is generally fome prejudice, party fpirit, or perfonal intereft, that leads people to contradict and deny what they are ignorant of.

Thefe Letters will be admired, in fpite of every objection which national prejudice or malevolence can make to them; and the more they are known, the more honour will they reflect on the prefent century, on their illuftrious Author, and on his country. The memory of the righteous ought to be enternized, and this monument of Ganganelli's fame will furvive beyond the blindnefs of prepoffeffion, and the clamour of envy.

The counterfeits, which multiply on all hands, and abound with errors, oblige me

to

to repeat, that the only correct edition is
that which is to be had at Lottin's junior,
Bookseller at Paris, signed with his name.

N. B. The counterfeits we speak of,
who have printed the Life of Clement XIV.
have had the folly to take their impression
from the first Edition, which is exceedingly imperfect, when compared with the
last; and this Life, which they have joined to the Two Volumes of Letters, they
have declared to be an Edition augmented
more than one third.

D 5 LET-

LETTERS, &c.

LETTER I.

TO M. DE CABANE, KNIGHT OF MALA.

SIR,

THE folitude which you have formed to yourfelf in your own breaft renders it unneceffary to feek any other. Cloifters are only to be preferred in proportion as the mind becomes more collected there; for the merits of a Monaftery are not in the walls.

The Convent of La Trappe which we have in Italy, to which you purpofe retiring, is not lefs ftrict than the one of the fame Order in France; but wherefore quit the world, while you can improve it? It will remain for ever wicked, if abandoned by all the good.

D 6

Befides,

Befides, is not the Order of Malta, in which you live, a religious Order, and capable of purifying you, if you difcharge your duty in it?

We ought to deliberate well before we take upon us a new load of obligations. The Gofpel is the beft guide for a Chriftian; and before we bury ourfelves in folitude, the vocation ought to be well weighed.

There is fomething extraordinary in whatever takes us out of the common road of life; and in embracing the life of a Monk, we ought to dread fome illufion. I truely honour the Monks who follow the inftitutions of the Chartreufe and La Trappe, but only a few of thefe Orders are wanted. Befides the difficulty of finding a great number of Religious truely fervent, they ought to be apprehenfive of injuring the ftate, by rendering themfelves ufelefs members of fociety. We are not born Monks, we are born Citizens. The world requires people to contribute to its harmony, to make empires flourifh by their talents, by their labour, and their morals.

Thefe

Thefe profound folitudes, which fhow no exterior figns of life, are only graves. St. Anthony, who lived long in the defert, did not make a vow to remain always there. He quitted his retreat, and came into the middle of Alexandria to combat Arianifm, and difperfe the Arians; becaufe he was convinced that the ftate and the caufe of Religion were to be ferved by actions, more than by prayers. When he had accomplifhed the purpofe of his miffion, he returned to his Hermitage, in forrow for having preferved the little blood which old age had ftill left in his veins, and that he had not fuffered martyrdom.

When at La Trappe, it is true, you will pray to God day and night; but cannot you direct your thoughts continually to him, though in the middle of the world? It is not in words that the merit of prayer confifts; our fovereign Lawgiver tells us himfelf, that it is not the multitude of words which can obtain for us the favour of Heaven.

Many refpectable Writers have not hefitated to impute the remiffnefs in Monafteries

nafteries to a tirefome repetition of forms of devotion. They thought, with reafon, that the attention could not be preferved during too long prayers, and that bodily labour is of more advantage than continual pfalm-finging.

The world would not have exclaimed fo much againft the Monks, if they had been feen ufefully employed. The memory of thofe who cultivated wilds, and enriched cities with fkilful productions, or afcertained hiftorical facts or the dates of events, are ftill refpected.

The Benedictines of the learned Congregation of St. Maur in France, which we vulgarly call Maurini, have acquired lafting honour by the publication of a number of works both curious and ufeful. The celebrated P. Montfaucon, who is one of the greateft ornaments, filled all Italy with the fame of his learning, when he dedicated his application entirely to the ftudy of antiquity.

St. Bernard, the reformer of fo many Monafteries which are governed by his inftitutions, rendered himfelf very ufeful,

both

both to Religion and his country; not when he preached up the Crufades, which could only be juftified by the intention; but when he gave ufeful advice both to Popes and Kings, and compofed his immortal works. He had not become a Father of the Church, if he had done nothing but pray.

Father Mabillon, in his famous treatife on Monaftic Studies, appears to me to have fully triumphed over the Abbé de Rancé, who afferts that Monks fhould only be occupied in contemplation and pfalmody. The deftiny of man is to labour. *There is but one ftep from a fpeculative to an idle life,* faid Cardinal Paleotti, and nothing is more eafy than to pafs the line.

You will do more good by relieving the poor, and comforting them by your counfels, than by burying yourfelf in a Monaftery. John the Baptift, who was the greateft amongft men, quitted the defert to declare the kingdom of God was approaching, and to baptife on the banks of Jordan.

Do not imagine, my dear Sir, that in fpeaking of a ufeful life, I want to make an apology for the religious Mendicants, at

4   the

the expence of the Anchorets. Every Order has its rules; and the maxim here fhould be, *that he who doth not eat flefh, fhould not defpife him who doth:* but I own I efteem the Brother Minors more, becaufe they join the active life of Martha, to the con·templative one of Mary; and I believe, whatever certain enthufiafts may fay, the former is much the more meritorious.

St. Benedict was fenfible that we ought to be ufeful to our country, and in confequence inftituted a feminary for Gentlemen at Mont-Caffino. He knew what fort of laws the love of our neighbour infpires.

If, however in fpite of all I have faid, you ftill feel a fecret infpiration which calls you to the monaftic life, you may do what you think proper; for I fhould be afraid to oppofe the will of God, who leads his fervants as he pleafeth, and often by uncommon means.

I wifh I could be with you at Tivoli, to meditate in fight of that famous Cafcade, which, dividing into a thoufand different torrents,

torrents, and falling with the greateſt im-
petuoſity, preſents to the mind a lively
picture of this world, and its various agi-
tations.

I wiſh you agreeable holidays, and am,
more than Ciceronian eloquence can ex-
preſs, Sir,

Your moſt humble, &c.

Fr. L. Ganganelli.

At the Convent of the Holy Apostles,
    29th Oct. 1747.

My humble reſpects to the moſt worthy
Biſhop.

LETTER II.

TO THE ABBE FERGHEN.

Mons. Abbe,

YOU cannot do better to divert yourſelf from your troubles and embar-
raſſment than to viſit Italy. Every well-
informed man owes an homage to this
country, ſo deſervedly boaſted of; and it
will

will give me inexpreffible fatisfaction to fee you here.

The firft object that ftrikes you will be the great bulwarks given us by Nature, in the Alps and Appennines, which feparate us from France, and have occafioned our being ftiled Tramontanes by that nation. They are a majeftick range of mountains, which ferve as a frame to the magnificent picture within them.

Torrents, rivulets, and rivers, without reckoning the feas, are objects which prefent the moft curious and interefting points of view to foreigners, and efpecially to painters. Nothing can be more agreeeable than the moft fertile foil in the fineft climate, every where interfected with ftreams of running water, and every where peopled with villages, or ornamented with fuperb cities.—Such a country is Italy!

If agriculture was held in equal efteem with architecture; if the country was not divided into fuch a number of governments, all of different forms, and almoft all weak, and of little extent; mifery would

not

not be found by the fide of magnificence, and induftry without activity; but unfortunately we are more engaged in the embellifhment of cities, than in the culture of the country; and uncultivated lands every where reproach the idlenefs of the people.

If you begin your route at Venice, you will fee a city very fingular from its fituation;—it refembles a great fhip refting upon the waters, and which cannot be approached but by boats.

The fingularity of its fituation is not the only thing that will furprife you.—The inhabitants in mafque for four or five months in the year—the laws of a defpotick government, which allow the greateft liberty in their amufements; the rights of a Sovereign without authority; the cuftoms of a people who dread even his fhadow, and yet enjoy the greateft tranquillity, form inconfiftencies, which in a very extraordinary manner muft affect foreigners. There is fcarcely a Venetian who is not eloquent; – collections have been made of the *bons mots* of their Gondoliers, replete with true Attick falt.

                                          Ferrara

Ferrara difplays a vaft and beautiful folitude within its walls, almoft as filent as
the tomb of Ariofto, who was buried there.

Bologna prefents another kind of picture; there the Sciences are familiar, even
to the Sex *; who appear with dignity in
the Schools and Academies, and have tro-
phies frequently erected to them. A thoufand different paintings will gratify your
mind and eyes, and the converfation of
the inhabitants will delight you.

You will then pafs through a multitude
of fmall towns, in the fpace of more than
a hundred leagues, each of which has its
Theatre; its Cafin *(a rendezvous for the
nobility)* a man of learning, or fome Poet,
who employ themfelves according to their
tafte or their leifure.

You will vifit Loretto, made famous by
the great concourfe of pilgrims from other
countries, and the treafures with which the
church is magnificently enriched.

You

* This expreffion is not diftinguifhed in the original
by a gender: for there is a certain peculiar politenefs
in the Italian and French languages, that whenever
the word *fex* is ufed abfolutely and irrelatively, it is
always to be underftood of the *female*.

You will then defcry Rome, which may be feen a thoufand years, and always with new pleafure. The city, fituated upon feven hills, which the ancients called the Seven Miftreffes of the World, feems from thence to command the univerfe, and boldly to fay to mankind, that fhe is the Queen and the Capital.

You will call to mind the ancient Romans, the remembrance of whom can never be effaced, on cafting an eye on the famous Tiber, which has been fo often mentioned, and which has been fo frequently fwelled by their own blood, and that of their enemies.

You will be in extacy at the fight of St. Peter's, which Artifts fay is the wonder of the world; being infinitely fuperior to the St. Sophia at Conftantinople, St. Paul's at London, or even the temple of Solomon.

It is a ftructure which extends itfelf as you furvey it, where the whole feems to be immenfe, while every member of it appears to preferve its due proportion. The paintings are exquifite, the monumental fculptures breathe, and you will imagine that you fee the New Jerufalem come down

2   from

from Heaven, which St. John fpeaks of in the Revelations.

You will find, both in the great and in the detail of the Vatican, which was erected on the ruins of falfe oracles, beauties of every kind that will tire your eyes, while they at the fame time charm you. Here Raphael and Michael Angelo, fometimes in a fublime, fometimes in a pathetick manner, have difplayed the mafter-pieces of their genius; by expreffing in the moft lively language the whole energy of their fouls; and here the fcience and genius of all the writers in the world are depofited, in the multitude of works which compofe that rich and immenfe library.

Churches, palaces, publick fquares, pyramids, obelifks, pillars, galleries, grand fronts of buildings, theatres, fountains, gardens, views, all, all will declare to you that you are at Rome; and every thing will attach you to it, as to the city, which of all others has been the moft univerfally admired. You will not, indeed, meet with that French elegance which prefers the beautiful to the fublime; but you

will

will be amply recompenfed by thofe ftriking views that every inftant muft excite
your admiration.

Laftly, in all the figures of painting or
of fculpture, both ancient and modern, you
will fee a new creation, and almoft think
it animated. The Academy of Painting,
filled with French ftudents, will fhow you
fome who are deftined to become great Mafters in their profeffion, and who by coming to ftudy here do honour to Italy.

You will admire the grandeur and fimplicity of the Head of the Church, the
fervant of fervants in the order of humility, and the firft of men in the eyes of the
Faithful. The Cardinals who furround
him will reprefent to you the twenty-four
old men who encircle the throne of the
Lamb, whom you will find equally modeft
in their manners, and edifying in their
morals.

But thefe great and pleafing objects will
be difgraced by the difgufting fight of
groupes of Mendicants, whom Rome im-
properly fupports, by beftowing mifappli-
ed charity, inftead of employing them in
ufeful

uſeful labours: thus it is that the thorn is ſeen with the roſe, and vice too frequently by the ſide of virtue.

But if you wiſh to ſee Rome in all her ſplendour, endeavour to be there by the feaſt of St. Peter. The illumination of the Church begins with a gentle light, which you may eaſily miſtake for the reflection of the ſetting ſun: it then ſends forth ſome pieces of beautiful architecture, and afterwards finiſhes with waving flames, which make a moving picture, that laſts till daybreak. All this is attended with double fire-works, the ſplendour of which is ſo bright, that you would think the ſtars had fallen from the Heavens, and burſt upon the earth.

I do not mention to you the ſtrange metamorphoſis which has placed the Order of St. Francis even in the Capitol, and has produced a new Rome from the ruins of the old; to ſhow the world that Chriſtianity is truely the work of God, and that he has ſubdued the moſt-famous conquerors to eſtabliſh it in the very centre of their empire.

If

If the modern Romans do not appear warlike, it is becaufe the nature or principle of their government does not infpire them with valour; but they have the feed of every virtue, and make as good foldiers as any when they carry arms under a foreign power. It is certain that they have a great fhare of genius, a fingular aptitude in acquiring the Sciences; and you would imagine they were born Harlequins, fo expreffive are they in their geftures, even from their infancy.

You will next travel by the famous Appian Way, which from its age is become wretchedly inconvenient, and you will arrive at Naples, the Parthenope of the Ancients, where the afhes of Virgil are depofited, and where you will fee a laurel growing, which could not poffibly be better placed.

Mount Vefuvius on one fide, and the Elyfian Fields on the other, prefent a moft fingular and contrafted view; and after being fatisfied with this delightful profpect, you will find yourfelf furrounded by a multitude of Neapolitans, lively and ingenious, but too much addicted to pleafure

Vol. I.   E   and

and idlenefs, to become what they otherwife might be capable of. Naples would
be a delightful place, if it was not for the
multitudé of the lower populace, who have
the appearance of unhappy wretches, or
banditti, though often without being either
the one or the other.

The Churches are magnificently decorated, but their architecture is in a wretched tafte, and by no means comparable to
the Roman. You will have a fingular pleafure in traverfing the environs of this town,
which is moft delightful, from its delicious
fruits, charming views, and fine fituations.
You will penetrate into the famous fubter-
ranean city of Herculaneum, which was
fwallowed up in a former age by an erup-
tion of Mount Vefuvius. If the mountain happens to be raging, you will fee torrents of fire iffuing from its bowels, and
majeftically overfpreading the country.
You will fee a collection of whatever has
been recovered out of Herculaneum, at
Portici; and the environs of Puzzuolo,
fung by the Prince of Poets, will infpire
you with a true paffion for Poetry.

You

You fhould walk with the Æneid in your hand, and compare the cave of the Cumæan Sybil and Acheron with what Virgil has faid of them.

You will return by Caferta, which from its decorations, marbles, extent, and aqueducts worthy of ancient Rome, is the fineft place in Europe; and you will make a vifit to Mount Caffino, where the fpirit of St. Benedict has fubfifted uninterruptedly, above a dozen ages, in fpite of the immenfe riches of that fuperb monaftery.

Florence, from whence the fine arts have iffued, and where their moft magnificent mafter-pieces are depofited, will prefent other objects to your view. There you will admire a city, which according to the remark of a Portuguefe, *fhould only be fhown on Sundays*, it is fo handfome, and fo beautifully decorated. You will every where trace the fplendour and elegance of the family of Medici, infcribed in the Annals of Tafte as the reftorers of the fine arts.

Leghorn is a well inhabited fea-port, of great advantage to Tufcany. Pifa always

has

has men of learning, in every fcience, in its Schools. Sienna, remarkable for the purity of its air and language, will intereft you in a very fingular manner. Parma, placed in the midft of fertile paftures, will fhow you a theatre which can contain fourteen thoufand people, and where every one can hear what is faid, though fpoken in a whifper. Placentia will appear to you worthy of the name it bears, as its delightful fituation muft captivate every traveller.

You will not forgèt Modena, as it is the country of the famous Muratori, and a city celebrated for the name which it has given to its fovereigns.

You will find at Milan the fecond church in Italy, for fize and beauty: more than a thoufand marble ftatues decorate its outfide, and it would be a mafter-piece, if it had a proportionable front. The fociety of its inhabitants is quite agreeable, ever fince it was befieged by the French. They live there as they do in Paris, and every thing, even to the hofpitals and buryinggrounds, prefents an air of fplendour. The

Ambrofian

Ambrofian Library muft attract the Literati; and the Ambrofian ritual no lefs engage the Ecclefiaftick, who wifhes to know the ufages of the Church as well as thofe of antiquity.

The Borromean Ifles will next attract your curiofity, from the accounts you muft have had of them. Placed in the middle of a delightful lake, they prefent to your view whatever is magnificent or gay in gardens.

Genoa will appear to you truely fuperb in its Churches and Palaces. There you will fee a port famous for its commerce, and the refort of ftrangers. You will fee a Doge changed almoft as often as the Superiors of Communities, and with fcarce any greater authority.

And laftly Turin, the refidence of a Court where the Virtues have long inhabited, will charm you with the regularity of its buildings, the beauty of its fquares, the ftraightnefs of its ftreets, and the fpirit of the people; and there you will agreeably conclude your travels.

E 3   I have

I have been juft making the tour of Italy, moft rapidly and at a little expence as you fee, to invite you to it in reality;—it is fufficient to *fketch* paintings to fuch a mafter as you.

I make no mention of our morals to you; they are not more corrupt, than among other people, let Malice fay what it will; they vary only their fhades according to the difference of the governments.—The Roman does not refemble the Genoefe, nor the Venetian the Neapolitan; but you may fay of Italy, as of the whole world, that, with fome little diftinctions, it is here, as it is there, *a little good, and a little bad.*

I do not attempt to prejudice you in favour of the agreeablenefs of the Italians, nor of their love of the Arts and Sciences: you will very foon perceive it when you come among them; you of all men, with whom one is delighted to converfe, and one whom it will always be a pleafure to fay, that one is his moft humble and moft obedient fervant.

I have taken the opportunity of a leifure moment, to give you fome idea of my
country;

country; it is only a coarfe daubing, which in another hand would have been a beautiful miniature: the fubject deferves it, but my pencil is not fufficiently delicate for the execution.

ROME, 12th Nov. 1756.

LETTER III.

TO ONE OF HIS SISTERS.

THE lofs which we have had of fo many relations and friends, my dear Sifter, declares to us that this life is only borrowed, and that God alone effentially poffeffeth immortality. What ought to be our comfort is, that we fhall be re-united in, if we attach ourfelves conftantly to, Him.

The troubles you fpeak of ought to be more precious than pleafures, if you have faith. Calvary is in this world the general ftation of a Chriftian; and if he fometimes mounts upon Tabor, it is only for an inftant.

My health continues with its ufual vigour, becaufe I neither live too fparing,

E 4   nor

nor too full; my ſtomach is ſometimes inclined to be ſick, but I tell it that I have
not leiſure, and it leaves me in quiet.
Study abſorbs thoſe trifling inconveniencies which mankind complain of ſo frequently. It often happens that we are in-
diſpoſed, thro'idleneſs;—many women are
ſick, without knowing where their complaint lies, becauſe they have nothing to do:
they are tired of being too well, and this
ſatiety is oppreſſive to people of faſhion.

I am very glad to have ſuch good accounts of little Michael. It is a plant which
will produce excellent fruit, if carefully
cultivated. All depends upon a happy culture; we become every thing or nothing,
according to the education we receive.

You regret that we do not ſee one another; but neither our figures nor our
words form our friendſhip. Provided our
affections and thoughts unite us, what
ſignifies our perſons being at a diſtance?
When we love one another in God, we
ſee one another always, for God is every
where: he ought to be the centre of all
our ſentiments, as he is of our ſouls.

I em-

I embrace you moſt cordially, and ſet an high value on your Letters; they recal the memory of a Father I knew but too little, and of a Mother whoſe life was a conſtant leſſon of virtue. I have never failed to remember them at the altar, nor you, my dear ſiſter, to whom I am beyond all expreſſion,

A moſt humble and affectionate, &c.

LETTER IV.

TO MONSIGNOR BOUGAT, PRIVATE CHAMBERLAIN TO HIS HOLINESS.

MY LORD,

I WILL not fail to attend your kind invitation, as from one in whom ſenſe, knowledge, and chearfulneſs are happily united. If ever melancholy ſhould happen to lay hold of me, I ſhall reſcue myſelf from it by your agreeable converſe, of which Benedict XIV. ſo well knew the value, and which would have made the ſame impreſſion upon Saul, as David's harp. You have a talent for narration ſo

E 5 rapid

rapid and engaging, that even trifles, from the turn you give them, become matter of folid converfation.

It is a long time fince we met at Mount-Trinity. Our Fathers the French Minims are worthy of frequent vifits: one who loves either fcience or fociety muft be fond of their company; and this attachment grows ftronger, the longer you are acquainted with them.

When you come to fee me, I will fhow you my reflections upon a caufe in which you are interefted. There are of all kinds in the Holy Office; fome to make us laugh, and others to make us figh: but don't be afraid, I fhall not read any of the latter caft to you. The great art of paffing agreeably through life, is to confult people's taftes and inclinations.

Chearfulnefs is the true medicine for the ftudious; the mind **and** heart require **to** be dilated, when they have been contracted by too great affiduity. Bloffoming **is as** neceffary to the human mind as **to** trees, to make it recover its verdure, and flourifh; but there are people, who like

rofe-buds

rofe-buds unblown prefent nothing to your view but bark and prickles. When I meet with fuch perfons I keep filence, and pafs off from them as faft as poffible, for fear of being fcratched.

Chearfulnefs retards old age; there is ever an enlivening fpirit which accompanies gaiety, inftead of the palenefs and wrinkles that are the effect of care.

Benedict XIV. would not enjoy fuch good health, if he were not always in good humour:—he lays down his pen or his book, often to indulge his livelinefs of imagination, and by this means prevents his ftudies from becoming a fatigue to him.

You are in the right to graft the Italian gaiety upon the French—it is the way to live to a hundred. That you may do fo I fincerely wifh, for I am more than I can tell,

My Lord,

Your moft humble, &c.

LETTER V.

TO THE MOST REVEREND ABBE OF MONTE
CASSINO.

MOST REV. SIR,

YOU do me too much honour in con-
sulting me about the dates of your
two manuscripts. I believe them to be of
the ninth century, by comparing the characters in which they are written, with those
of that age; and besides there is one of our
Authors cited who lived at that time, whom
few people know, and whose fragments
upon the service of the Mass still exist.

It is very condescending in you to take
the feeble lights of a little Francifcan upon
that subject, while you are the Chief of an
Order perfectly versed in antiquity, and
which has given the most shining and honourable proofs of it, in all parts of the
world.

We should be great triflers, were it not
for the Benedictines, said Innocent XI.
(Odescalchi.) Besides their being an honour

to

to the Holy See, and the different Churches for whole ages, they have been the Fathers and prefervers of hiftory. With them Monarchs have found their moft auguft and interefting titles; and fcience and faith have been uninterruptedly preferved among them, while the thickeft clouds of ignorance feemed to overfhade the univerfe. Though rich and powerful, they have never been feen caballing in kingdoms, nor meddling in pernicious intrigues; on the contrary, they have proved of great affiftance to States: and we may fay, that notwithftanding all the wealth and honours they have received, publick gratitude has ftill left them unpaid.

If I can anfwer your intentions, I will moft willingly vifit that famous retreat which has produced fuch a number of faints and learned men. When we tread the ground inhabited by thefe great men, we imagine ourfelves fharers in their merits.

It is impoffible to add to the profound refpect with which I am, &c.

ROME, 5th March, 1748.

L E T-

LETTER VI.

TO MR. STUART, A SCOTCHMAN.

I HAVE followed you in idea, my dearest Sir, both by sea and upon the
Thames. While my travels in England are
only ideal, the populace will not insult me;
whereas were I to appear there in person,
and in my religious habit, God knows how
they might treat me. You must allow that
the Popes are good sort of men; for were
they to make reprisals, they would insist
that every Priest and Monk should have
leave to enter London in their habits, or
that no Englishman should be received into Rome. And who would suffer most?
You in the first place, my dear Sir, who
love to visit Italy from time to time; but
I protest to you, I should be still more
mortified than you, for I am most sincere-
ly attached to the English nation, and have
received both pleasure and advantage from
the conversation of its inhabitants, who
distinguish themselves by their zeal for the

3   culture

culture of arts and fciences. I am delighted with your famous Poets and your eminent Philofophers; in converfing with them
I find within me a certain elevation of
mind; methinks I grow fublime, and
perceive the world beneath me. I fometimes make nocturnal vifits to Newton,
and at a time when all nature fleeps, I wake
to read and admire him. No one like him
ever united fimplicity with fcience. His
character and genius were fuperior to pride
and oftentation.

I conclude, that at your return you will
bring me the little manufcript of Berke-
ley, that illuftrious *wrong-head*, who imagined there was nothing really *material*
in the world, and that all bodies were
merely *ideal*. What a view would it ex-
hibit of the human intellect, if the learned, who had hitherto bewildered themfelves
in the variety of opinions, fhould at laft
find themfelves of one mind, and that this
reafon, which has fo long remained *incog-
nito*, fhould come at length **to** enlighten
them with its beams! How furprifed and
mortified

mortified would they be, who had the vanity to imagine they were more than infpired! The world in all ages has been
the fcene of difputes and errors; and we
ought to think ourfelves happy amidft fo
many crowds of contradiction, to have fuch
an unerring light to lead us the right way:
I fpeak of the light of Revelation, which,
in fpite of all the efforts of infidelity, will
never be extinguifhed. Religion, like
the firmament, fometimes may appear obfcure to us, but at the fame time is not lefs
radiant. The paffions and fenfes are va-
pours which fpring from the womb of our
corruption, and intercept the ways of celeftial truth; but the man who reflects,
without being alarmed or aftonifhed waits
the return of a ferene and chearful fky.
We have feen the fogs difperfed which
were raifed by Celfus, Porphyry, Spinofa,
Collins, Bayle, &c. and we may be affured
that thofe of modern *philofophy* will fhare
the fame fate. In every age fome fingular
men have appeared, who fometimes by
violence, and fometimes by fanaticifm,
feemed to threaten the annihilation of

4   Chrifti-

Chriftianity; but they have paffed away like thofe tempefts which only ferve to fhow the face of Heaven more bright and ferene.

It is for want of principles of folid knowledge that fome men are dazzled by fophiftry; and the moft trivial objections appear unanfwerable to the ignorant. In Religion, every thing is united and combined; and the moment we quit our hold of the leaft truth, we plunge into a dark abyfs. Such men, inftead of concluding, from the view of the wonders they enjoy, that God can undoubtedly confer much greater happinefs after this life, judge that the Divinity, all powerful as he is, can go no farther, and that all this world is of courfe the *ne plus ultra* of his wifdom and power.

I fhould be curious to fee a work which could prove demonftratively (and fuch a one might be eafily compofed, provided the author was acquainted with natural philofophy and theology) that the world, fuch as we fee it, is a perfect riddle, of which there can be no folution without Religion.

Religion. It is Religion alone which can account to us for the immenfity of that Heaven, of which the unbeliever cannot divine the ufe; for the miferies which we fuffer, of which the Philofopher **cannot** affign the caufe; for the growing **defires** which agitate us, and whofe impetuofity we cannot calm.

We have frequently fketched out thefe great fubjects when we have difcourfed familiarly together, fometimes at the Villa Borghefe, and fometimes at the Villa Negroni. That time is paft, and **a** part of our lives with it, becaufe every thing paffeth away, except the fincere attachment with which **I am** with all my heart, my deareft Sir, &c.

ROME, 13th May, 1748.

LETTER VII.

TO SIGNOR BAZARDI

I Entreat you not to confult me about your fon's defign of embracing a monaftic life. If I tell you that he cannot do

better,

better, you will believe it to be the interefted language of a man fpeaking in favour of his Order: if I anfwer on the contrary, that he had better to think of it,
you will conclude it is the advice of a
Friar difgufted with his fituation, or convinced that the monaftick life is a life of
mifery. I will not therefore fay either
Yes, or No. Every object has two faces;
you fhould endeavour to difcover and adopt
that which is beft.

If I forefaw that a candidate would become eminent either in learning or piety,
I would employ every effort to determine
him; but when I do not know what may
happen, I am extremely referved, and
never advife any one to become a Friar.

I have the honour to be, &c.
Rome, 13th May, 1748.

LETTER VIII.
TO THE PRELATE CERATI.

I WILL not pardon your depriving the
Publick of a multitude of anecdotes,
which are familiar to you, and which, if
.collected,

collected would prove extremely interesting.—Henceforth when I see you, I will
take my pencil and write. What would
become of Science, were all the Learned to
pursue your plan? Conversation might be
brilliant, but reading would be the reverse.

Monsignor Cerati ought to reflect, that
while he speaks, he is only useful to those
who are about him; but if he would write
he might prove of service to the most distant. A book becomes the patrimony
of the whole world, and equally finds its
way to the Russian and the Italian. The
Pope ought to oblige you, under pain of
excommunication, to give the Publick, by
means of the press, all that knowledge
which you now withhold from them. But
perhaps, having seen foreign countries,
you may have become such a *Tramontane*,
as to think of eluding the judgment of a
Roman decree. Cardinal Porto Carrero
said to me lately, when speaking of you,
he has seen a great deal, read a great deal,
and retains every thing; but that will be of
no use to us, because he will carry his know-
ledge with him to the other world.

Too

Too much has been written, and I am grieved when I reflect upon the numerous productions of licentious fpirits; but we fhould never think that too much could be written, if the authors produce the excellent things which you know.—As for me, I will have it printed, that I cannot admire you too much, nor repeat too often how much I have the honour to be, &c.

LETTER IX.

TO THE MARQUIS CLERICI, A MILANSE.

ALLOW me to inform you, that Jaques Piovi is in the greateft mifery. I do not acquaint you with his being one of the Pope's foldiers, for that would be a poor title of recommendation to an Auftrian Officer: but I remind you of his having fix children; that he has kept his bed thefe nine months; and laftly that he is your god-fon.

Generofity, which chiefly marks your character, and which only feeks opportunities

nities of giving, has here an opportunity of being gratified. If you were one of thofe ordinary fouls who never obliged but with reluctance, I fhould not think of importuning you. I do not love **to extort** benefits; I wifh them to flow freely from their fource, and to have their principle in magnanimity.

I think I fee you fmile at the different complexion of this letter from thofe **daily** written to you by the gentlemen of your own profeffion. The fignature of *Frere Ganganelli* can have no **other** merit in your eyes, except that of fhowing with what profound refpect I have the honour **to be,** &c.

ROME, 9th September, 1748.

L E T-

LETTER X.

TO MADAM ***.

TRUE devotion, Madam, neither confifts in a carelefs air, nor in a brown habit. Moft votaries imagine, tho' I don't know why, that clothes of a dark colour pleafe the celeftial beings more than thofe of a lighter and more lively hue: yet we find the Angels are always painted either in white or blew. I do not love oftentatious piety; modefty does not depend upon colours; if it be decent in drefs and manner, it is what it really ought to be.

Obferve, moreover, that the lady who talks fcandal in an affembly, or appears peevifh, or in an ill humour againft mankind, is moft frequently dreffed in brown. Singularity is fo little allied to true devotion, that we are ordered in the Gofpel to wafh our faces when we faft, that we may not appear remarkable.

I am therefore of opinion, Madam, that you fhould make no alteration in the form

or

or colour of your drefs. Let every thought
and every action, be directed to the honour of God; for that is the fum of Religion.

Had it not been for the ill conduct of
the votaries of Religion, it would not have
been expofed to fo much ridicule from the
men of the world. Almoft always inflam-
ed with bitter zeal, they are never fatisfied
except with themfelves; and they would
have every one to fubmit to their whims,
becaufe their piety is often the effect only
of caprice.

Every perfon who is truly pious, is patient, gentle and humble; unfufpecting of
ill, never fplenetick, and conceals when he
cannot excufe the faul.s of his neighbour.
Every truely pious perfon *laughs with thofe*
that laugh, and weeps with thofe that weep,
according to the advice of St. Paul, *to be*
wife with fobernefs, becaufe there fhould be
temperance in all things.

In fine true devotion is charity, and
without it nothing we can do is of ufe to
falvation. Falfe devotees do little lefs
injury to the caufe of Religion, than the
openly

openly prophane. Always ready to kindle
againſt thoſe who do not agree with them
in their humours and opinions, they are
agitated by a reſtleſs, impetuous, perſecut-
ing zeal, and are commonly either fanati-
cal or ſuperſtitious, hypocrites or ignorant.
Jeſus Chriſt does not ſpare them in the
Goſpel, that he may teach us to be on our
guard againſt them.

When you find, Madam, that there is
neither rancour in your heart, nor pride in
your mind, nor ſingularity in your actions,
and that you obſerve the precepts of God
and his church without affectation or trifling, you may then believe you are in the
way of ſalvation.

Above all things, make your domeſtics
happy by abſtaining from tormenting them
They are counterparts of ourſelves, and
we ſhould conſtantly lighten their yoke ;—
the way to be well ſerved, is to have always a ſerene countenance. True piety is
at all times tranquil, while falſe devotion
is inceſſantly varying.

Support your nieces according to their rank, but do not exact of them to do precisely as you do, because you have a particular turn for mortification.

This article would require a whole letter. Young people are often disgusted with piety, because too great perfection is required; and works of penitence even tire ourselves, when they are not moderate. The common way of life is the most certain, though perhaps not the most perfect :—it is being too violent, to forbid all visiting and relaxation. Take care that your ghostly father be not too mystical, and that his instructions do not end in making you scrupulous, rather than a good Christian.

Does piety require us to be self-tormentors! Religion teaches us what we should do, and what we ought to believe; and there can be no better instructor than the Gospel. Mingle solitude with society, and contract acquaintance with such only as will neither lead you to melancholy, nor to dissipation.

Vary

Vary your reading. There are fome books for recreation, which may fucceed the more ferious. St. Paul, in giving rules for decent converfation, permits us to fay things that are chearful and agreeable; *quæcunque amabilia.*

To imagine we were always offending, were to ferve God like a flave. The yoke of the Lord is eafy, and his burthen is light. *Love God*, fays St. Auguftine, *and do what thou wilt*; becaufe then you will do nothing but what is agreeable to him, and you will act with refpect to him, as a fon towards a father whom he loves.

Above all things, be charitable; and the more fo, as you are in a fituation to affift the poor. Religion has humanity for a bafis, and they who are not charitable cannot be chriftians.

I do not by any means advife you to give to communities; befides that they do not want it, it is not juft to impoverifh families to enrich them. There is a continual outcry againft the rapacioufnefs of Monks, and you fhould not give occafion for new complaints upon that fubject. Our

repu-

reputation ought to be our greateſt riches, which ſhould be founded on diſintereſted-neſs, and the practice of every virtue.

Although a friend to my profeſſion, I ſhall never engage any one to make preſents to us; nor perſuade any body to become a Monk: I dread giving room for reproach and repentance, as I dread tiring you, ſhould I prolong this epiſtle, which has no other merit in my eyes, than the opportunity it procures me of aſſuring you of the reſpect with which I have the honour to be,

Madam, &c.

Rome, 2 Jan. 1749.

LETTER XI.

TO THE REV. FATHER ***, A FRANCISCAN
FRIAR.

MY DEAR FRIEND,

FOR three days together I have been
scribbling over all that you seem to
desire. I have endeavoured to introduce
into this discourse, the pathetick, the sublime, the simple, and the moderate, so as
to have where-withal to please different
tastes. You must endeavour not only to
commit it exactly to your memory, but to
pronounce it well ;—not merely for yourself, but likewise for your hearers, who
will be both numerous and respectable.

This little work will favour of haste,
but then it will have the more fire. My
imagination kindles like a Volcano, when
I am exceedingly hurried ; I collect all my
ideas, thoughts, perceptions, and sentiments, and the whole together bubbles in
my head and upon my paper, most sur-
prisingly.

F 3   Not-

Notwithſtanding the warmth which you will find in this production, I have arranged it as well as I could. I ſhall be ſatisfied with it, if you are ſatisfied, and I moſt earneſtly wiſh it.

The war burns more fiercely than ever, and they write me from Flanders, that the towns fall like tiles in a ſtorm. God ſend the French may always prove conquerors! You know how much I love that nation, and how much I intereſt myſelf in its ſucceſs. I ſhould certainly have been born in France :—it is the turn of my heart and mind which makes me think ſo.

Do not tell any one that you have heard from me. The Monks are acute, and they will ſuſpect that your Diſcourſe came from me, if you by any means recal me to their m꞉n꞉ rance.

I am always wrapped up in my own thoughts, which are either open or reſerved, according to the work which Providence impoſes upon me, or accident produces. My day is often an unintelligible chaos – I muſt paſs from one taſk to another; and theſe extravagances are more unlike

unlike than white is to black, or day to night. I then throw myfelf into the vortex of the Brotherhood, talking and laughing *ab hoc & ab hac*, becaufe I muft renew my exiftence I am fo much exhaufted. I frequently leave the old folks to chat with the young ones, where we joke like children : it is the beft way of refrefhing ourfelves after quitting deep ftudy, and it was the method of the celebrated Muratori.

Adieu ! Love me, becaufe you ought, fince I am, as I have been, and always fhall be, your beft friend.

From the CONVENT of the HOLY APOSTLES.

LETTER XII.

TO A CANON OF OSIMO.

SIR,

RELIGION, which refided in the bofom of God from all eternity, produced itfelf the moment that the univerfe fprang from nothing, and came to take up

F 4 its

its abode in the heart of Adam. There was the firſt temple upon earth ; and it is from thence that the moſt fervent deſires are continually exhaled towards Heaven. Eve, formed in innocence as well as her huſband, partook of the incſtimable advantage of bleſſing every inſtant the Author of their being. The birds united their warblings, and all Nature applauded the heavenly concert.

Such was Religion, and ſuch its worſhip, till ſin came into the world to ſtain its purity—then Innocence fled away, and Penitence endeavoured to ſupply its place. Adam, baniſhed from an earthly paradiſe, found no longer any thing but briars and thorns, where he had formerly gathered the faireſt flowers and moſt excellent fruits.

The juſt Abel offered his own heart as a burnt-offering to God, and ſealed with his blood the love which he had for truth and juſtice. Noah, Lot, Abraham, Iſaac, and Jacob, ſerved as guides to one another, in obſerving the law of Nature, as the only Religion which at that time was pleaſing in the ſight of God.

Moſes

Mofes appeared like a new ftar feen
fhining upon Mount Sinai, at the fide of
the fun of Juftice; and the Ten Commandments were given him to be obeyed without any alteration. Thunder was the ex-
ternal fign of this new alliance, and the
Jewifh people became the depofitory of a
law written by Wifdom itfelf.

Notwithftanding the zeal of Mofes and
Jofhua, and all the leaders of the people
of God, the Chriftian Religion alone could
produce worfhippers in fpirit and in truth.
Every thing which was efteemed holy before that time, already belonged to it; and
when it was prefented to the world proceeding from the Incarnate Word, it was
eftablifhed on the ruins of Judaifm, like a
beloved daughter, *filia dilecta*, and it changed the face of the whole world.

Wicked defires were forbidden, as well
as wicked actions, and the pureft and moft
fublime virtues fprang from the blood of
a multitude of Martyrs.

The Church fucceeded the Synagogue,
and the Apoftles, who were its pillars, had
fucceffors who were to tranfmit their office

F 5

to

to the end of time. According to that
heavenly plan, and this divine œconomy,
the fubftance fucceeded to the fhadow;
for the old law was only the type of Jefus
Chrift; and the evidence of it after death,
will be the recompence of faith. God will
be feen as he is, and the faithful will reft
eternally with him.

Behold in what manner you fhould fet
out in your work upon Religion; go to its
fource, and fhow its excellence; afcend
with it to Heaven, from whence it defcend-
ed, and whither it will return.

Religion will never be perfectly eftablifhed till it has no other principle but
Charity; for neither knowledge nor exterior magnificence conftitute its merit, but
the love of God alone. It is the bafis of
our worfhip, and if we are not perfuaded of
this truth, we are only the images of virtue.

I confider Religion as a chain, of which
God is the firft link, and which reacheth
to eternity. Without this tie every thing
is diffolved and overthrown—men are
creatures only deferving of contempt—
the univerfe not worth our attention; for it

is

is neither the fun nor the earth that makes
its merit, but the glory of being a part of
the Supreme Being; and, according to the
words of the Apoſtle, to ſubſiſt only in
Jeſus Chriſt—*Omnia per ipſum & in ipſo
conſtant*.

Admit nothing into your work which is
unworthy of your ſubjeɛt; and when you
meet in your way ſome famous unbeliever,
or celebrated hereſiarch, overthrow him with
that courage which truth inſpires, but
without virulence or oſtentation.

It is ſo pleaſing to ſupport the cauſe of
a religion which has united every teſti-
mony of Heaven and Earth in its favour,
that it ſhould not be defended but with
moderation. Flights of genius have nothing in common with truth. *It is ſufficient
to ſhow religion ſuch as it is,* ſaid the holy
Charles Borroméo, *to make the neceſſity of it
be known.* Men who would give up Religion, muſt either be reduced to eat acorns,
or return to their original ſtate of violence
and war.

I have ſtudied Religion more than forty-
five years, and am always more and more

ſtruck

ftruck with it.   It is too elevated to be of human invention, although the wicked fay it is.   Fill your mind with the fpirit of God before you begin to write, that you may not make ufe of vain words.   Where the heart is not perfectly confenting with the pen which expreffeth holy truths, it is feldom that the reader can be affected.   **Pe-netrate** their fouls with the fame fpirit which God himfelf brought upon earth, and **your** book will produce wonderful effects.

What has made *The Imitation of Jefus Chrift* fo valuable and affecting, is, that the Author (Gerfen, Abbé of Verceil in Italy) has transfufed into it all that holy charity with which he himfelf was divinely animated.

Gerfon is commonly confounded with Gerfen ; neverthelefs it is eafy to prove, that neither Gerfon nor Thomas à Kempis were the authors of that matchlefs book ; and this I own gives me infinite pleafure, becaufe I am delighted with the thought of fuch an excellent work being written by an Italian.   There is an evident proof in the

the fifth Chapter of the fourth Book, that it was not a Frenchman who wrote *The Imitation.* It is there expreffed, that the Prieft clothed in his facerdotal habit carries the crofs of Jefus Chrift before him; now all the world knows, that the Chafubles * in France differ from thofe in Italy, in this, that they have the crofs upon their backs; but I will not **write a** differtation, being content to affure you that I am, &c.

Rome, 6th Feb. 1749.

LETTER XIII.

TO COUNT ALGAROTTI.

THE Pope is always great, and always agreeable by his *bons mots.* He faid the other day, that he always loved you, and it would be a great pleafure to him to fee you again. He fpeaks of the King of Pruffia with admiration; and it muft be owned that he is a Monarch whofe hiftory will make one of the nobleft monuments of the eighteenth century. Con-

* Chafubles are a kind of Copes which the Priefts wear at Mafs.

fefs that I am very generous, for he laughs at the Court of Rome and the Monks, as much as poffible.

Your laft letter is full of philofophy :— I have fhown it to our common friends, who find in it the fire of Italy, with the phlegm of Germany. This mixture works wonders in the eyes of men of fenfe and genius.

Cardinal Quirini will not be fatisfied without having you fome time at Brefcia; he told me one day, that he would invite you to come and confecrate his library; he is enriching it as much as he can, doubt-lefs that it may be worthy of you.

You will enliven Bologna when you re-turn—the Mufes are not afleep, but they are not fo animated as they were formerly; fuch a fpirit as your's is wanted to electrify the Academicians.

Rome does not make me forget that town where I paffed fo much time. The rememberance of the learned men I knew there, renders it always prefent. If the will of the Pontiff did not keep me tied here, I would willingly go and end my days there,

there, feeing nothing in the career which I have to pafs, that can be more agreeable or more advantageous. I fhould poffefs myfelf, and be perfectly content, though it be but a very fmall poffeffion. The domain of my knowledge is of fo little extent, that by reducing myfelf within my own fphere, I am confined to the fimpleft mediocrity.

Natural Philofophy tells me from time to time, that I neglect her.—I anfwer, I am a greater lofer than you. But what would you have me do? Theology is become my fovereign, and I muft obey her without referve. They who do not know her, fuppofe her to be a chimera, or an idol; but for me, who confider her under every relation, and in her whole extent, I acknowledge her to be the true light of the foul, and the life of the Elect. Nothing that flows from God, nothing that he fays, nothing that relates to him, can be trifling or indifferent. There is no harm in my preaching to a Philofopher who does not commonly go to church, and who has not been fanctified by his refidence at Potzdam.

I   There

There are three men of you there, whofe talents would be of great fervice to Religion, if you would change their direction. You, Monf. Voltaire, and Monf. Maupertuis; but that is not the **ton** of the prefent age, and you will be in the **fafhion**.

In expectation of this miracle, which God can bring about fome time or other, although **there is** little appearance of it, I have the honour to be with the higheft refpect, &c.

LETTER XIV.

TO THE ABBE LAMI.

I WOULD gladly revifit Frefcati, that delightful dwelling, where the multitude of *jets d'eau*, fhooting up towards Heaven without interruption, is a lively image of the elevation and humiliation of weak mortals :—I have tired my limbs and my eyes by walking and obferving them. The country is not agreeable, but as we open the **two** great books of botany

and

and aftronomy ; the one under our feet,
the other over our heads.

It is wonderful to obferve how the foul
is elevated one moment to a ftar, and the
next falls down to a grain of fand ; how it
expands over the immenfity of the Heavens,
and how it fhrinks back upon itfelf ; how
it analyfes the light, antomifes an infect ;
how inceffant are its wifhes, yet how
limited its faculties ! We may fay then
with Danté, *that the foul is the greateft wonder
of the univerfe.*

The ftudy of Nature is neceffary to know
the Author of Nature ; and the great Newton faid, that an Aftronomer or Anatomift
abfolutely could not be an Atheift. The
air is not perceivable, although we every
where feel its influence ; it is an image of
God himfelf, who, though invifible, informs us every inftant of his prefence and
action.

I have recovered a new life in the country to dedicate it more than ever to bufinefs. One of the ancients faid, that Death
fhould find an Emperor ftanding ; and I
add, that he fhould find a Counfellor of the
Holy

Holy Office with his pen in his hand. You will allow that I have not placed myself amifs.

That laft moment is approaching every inftant, and time is almoft nothing. The paft, the prefent, and the future are fo near each other, that one has not leifure to dif-tinguifh them. The year has fcarce begun its courfe when it is at an end.

I had never written a fingle word, nor made a fingle comma, without looking upon it as a point cut off from my life. This manner of thinking is the beft means of repelling Ambition; but I do not believe that fhe will ever come to knock at my gate. I defpife Fortune too much for her to make me any advances.

However, it is a fingular happinefs that I can affure you of all the attachment with which I am, &c.

Rome, 12th October, 1749.

LETTER XV.

TO A CARMELITE NUN.

IT appears, my reverend Mother, that
God Almighty has chosen mountains as
the propereſt places for diſplaying his glory
and his mercy. I ſee by the Scriptures, that
Mount Sinai, Mount Thabor, the Mount
of Olives, and Mount Calvary, were the
moſt privileged ſpots in the world, on account of the miracles which were wrought
there: and I ſee in the Hiſtory of the
Church, Mount Caſſino and Mount Carmel
giving birth to two Orders, which do honour to Religion by their penitence.

Holy Thereſa, your illuſtrious Refor-
matrix, is one of the greateſt ſouls that
God hath raiſed up for the good of Chriſtianity: a parent of the Church for her
knowledge and writings; and a model of
penitence by her auſterities. There is not
a cloud which can in the leaſt obſcure her
actions. Always with God to ſtudy him:
always

always with the faithful to inftruct them ; and always in the fame degree of perfec- tion ; fhe is a prodigy of fcience and of fanctity.

Her works are not fufficiently known ; —the beft is undoubtedly the wonderful harmony which reigns among fo many illuftrious females, to whom fhe is a fup- port and model.

You have no occafion for any inftruc- tions, my reverend Mother, but what have been given by this great Saint. She hath faid every thing, fhe hath forefeen every thing, and fhe hath taught every thing. The Nuns cannot choofe a better Di- rector ; and it is to her that they fhould addrefs themfelves, if their piety has none of thofe keen affections which hurt true devotion.

Confult holy Therefa then, and not Bro- ther Ganganelli, who is the weakeft perfon I know. I can only glean after thofe who have reaped a full harveft ; and all the correfpondence that I can have with you, is to beg that you will be fo good as to pray for me. The prayers of the Carmelites

are

are the moſt agreeable perfume which can
aſcend to the throne of God.   But not to
interrupt that ſilence any longer, which is
preſcribed you, I ſhall content myſelf with
adding to this letter the reſpect with which
I ſhall be, all my life,

                    Your moſt humble, &c.

At the CONVENT of the HOLY APOSTLES,
       19 June, 1749.

─────────────────────

L E T T E R XVI.

TO CARDINAL VALENTI, SECRETARY OF STATE.

MOST EMINENT,

THIS letter is the ſupplication of a
     poor Monk, for a poor Man, who is
leſs than nothing in the eyes of ſuch a Lord
as you ; but a ſubject worthy of all your
attention, if you look upon him with that
Chriſtian philoſophy which places mankind
on a level, and directs all your actions.

                              The

                3

The fubject in queftion is Dominic Baldi, a domeftick who has been long attached to your fervice, and who has been difmiffed for a fally of paffion. As he comes from the place where **I was born,** and I know him to have a number of good qualities, efpecially his fingular attachment to you, I venture to fupplicate you in his favour.

My Lord, you have a great foul, and I am fure of fuccefs, if you will only hearken a little—your heart will be my beft interceffor with you. Men are not angels—fervants have their faults, and fo have their mafters.

I would have follicited this favour in perfon; but probably I fhould have been obliged to wait in an ante-chamber, on account of the people and bufinefs which befet you, and I have not time to lofe. There are fo many burthens of every kind impofed upon me, that I have need of all my courage not to fink under them.

If

If you grant my requeſt, my gratitude
ſhall be as laſting and extenſive, as the
profound reſpect with which I am

Your Eminency's

Moſt humble, &c.

Rome, the 1ſt of the Month.

LETTER XVII.

TO THE SAME.

I AM quite vain that an atom ſhould
fix the attention of your Eminence,
and that a poor wretch, who had only ſuch
a pitiful recommendation as mine, ſhould
be received again into your ſervice. This
goodneſs does you the more honour, as it
ſhows you to be a great man without prejudices; that is to ſay, a phænomenon.

I have the honour to be, &c.

Rome, the 1ſt of the Month.

L E T.

LETTER XVIII.

TO THE PRELATE CERATI.

CHAINED down by my profeſſion, tormented with buſineſs, and hurried away by the times, I cannot diſpoſe my affairs ſo as to be able to join you. I am ſo much engaged, that I have only ſix hours in the day. I wiſh to God, that all thoſe whoſe time hangs heavy upon their hands could make a preſent of their ſpare moments to me: not that I might lead a longer life, but that I might give myſelf up to ſtudy more at my eaſe, without the dread of becoming too contemplative.

Your are happy in being at Florence, where you have no court to make except to monuments, libraries, or learned men, and where there is no danger of being ill received.

I will immediately ſend you the memorial you deſire;—it ſhall be written with all poſſible moderation, becauſe it is conformable with charity, and becauſe works

written

written with paffion, though they have truth on their fide, do no fort of good.

In fpite of all your eulogies on the plea-fures of gardening, it is impoffible for me to be fond of them; I know nothing but meadows and fields. When I have need of a walk, chance finds me a thoufand little charming paths, where I exceedingly love to wander.

The Pope only difcharges his duty, in vindicating the memory of Cardinal Nori. It would be cruel to declare a man a he-retick, becaufe he follows the opinions of the Auguftines or Thomifts; that is to fay, doctrines folemnly approved by the Church; but when we are impelled by fa-naticifm, we fee nothing, and become deaf to reafon.

The good Bifhop of Spoletto ftill enjoys excellent health; he writes to me with as much gaiety as if he were only twenty. He is like the Pope (Benedict XIV.) al-ways chearful.—He complains that the Hermits who live almoft under his eye are too diffipated—it is a growing evil in al-moft all the Communities—they no longer study but in extracts. Provided they have only the scarf-skin of the sciences, they think themselves great doctors. I don't know to what this will lead us, but I am afraid we shall insensibly fall back into the ignorance of the tenth century. Science is like the moon, which after being seen in full, shows only her half, and at last becomes entirely hid.

Sleep, which I must not neglect, tells me that we must part. What comforts me is that my friendship for you never sleeps, and that I am day and night irrevocably,

Your most humble, &c.

ROME, 8th July, 1749.

LETTER XIX.

TO COUNT ***.

SIR,

I WAS too much the friend of your father, and am too much your friend, to suffer you to go astray as you now do, without recalling you to yourself. Is it possible that that dear child whom I have seen so gentle, good, and virtuous in his

father's

father's houfe, has fo totally forgot what
he was, as to become rude, infolent, and
irreligious? It is with the utmoft difficulty I can perfuade myfelf that it is fo;
but I am fo often affured of it, and by the
company with whom you affociate, that I
can no longer doubt.

I beg of you to come and fee me, and in
the effufions of a heart which tenderly
loves you, I will fay to you, not what anger
infpires, not what prejudice fuggefts, not
what is bitter in reproaches, but all that
the fincereft attachment can dictate, to
withdraw you from that abyfs into which
bad company has hurried you.

. You will neither find me an imperious
monitor, nor an angry pedagogue, but a
friend, a brother, who will fpeak to you as
he would to himfelf, with the fame lenity,
and with the fame calmnefs. I know that
youth is fiery, and that there is great difficulty in efcaping from the ways of the
world, when we are rich, and given up to
paffions. But do not honour, decency,
reafon, and Religion fpeak more powerfully
than the appetites and fenfes?

What

What is man, my dear friend, if he takes no counsel but of his corrupted heart? Alas! I find within me, as well as you find in yourself, wherewithal to lead me astray, if I did not hearken to my conscience and my duty; for illusion and corruption are the only portions of humanity.

I expect you with the greatest impatience, to stretch forth my arms and embrace you. Do not startle at the sight of my cloister or my habit. On account of my profession, I ought to be the more charitable. We will bewail together the loss of a father who was so necessary to you; I will endeavour to give you such advice as to make him live again in you, by the excellence of your morals. Do not disgrace his memory by the scandal of a disorderly life.

There is nothing lost yet, if you will deign to hearken to me; for I am confident that the plan of life which I shall trace out to you, will restore every thing as it should be. Do not be afraid; I will not send you to do penance either with the Capuchins or the Chartreux, for I do not love violence. God will inspire us: God

does

does not abandon thofe who return to him.
I fhall not ftir abroad to-morrow, that I
may receive you.

LETTER XX.

TO THE SAME.

IS it poffible, my dear Sir, that you not
only did not come to me, as I requefted
you would, but that you took care to
be denied when I came to fee you? Alas!
what would your father fay, to whom you
promifed in his dying moments, that you
would place entire confidence in my advice, and that you would always make it
your duty to cultivate my friendfhip?
Once more, what would he fay? Am not
I the fame perfon who have carried you fo
often in my arms, who with the greateft
pleafure have feen you growing, who have
given you your firft inftructions, and to
whom you have teftified the ftrongeft attachment, on a thoufand occafions?

G 3　　　　Would

Would you have me fall upon my knees,
to induce you to reſtore to me your friendſhip? I will do ſo—nothing ſhall be too
much for me, when I am to recal a friend
to his duty.

If you had not a noble heart and a good
underſtanding, I ſhould deſpair of your
reformation, and of my own advice ; but
you have inherited a ſoul formed for virtue, and an uncommon ſagacity. Do you
imagine that it can be pleaſure to me to
find fault with you? None but falſe devotees find ſatisfaction in putting themſelves into a paſſion. I have happily read
the Goſpel, which is the rule both of your
conduct and mine, enough to know how
Jeſus Chriſt received ſinners, and how attentive we ought to be not to extinguiſh
the ſmoaking lamp, nor to break the bruiſ-
ed reed. I have not forgot that John the
Evangeliſt got on horſeback, notwithſtanding his advanced age, to ſearch after a
young man whom he had bred up, and
who avoided him. Beſides, have not you
long known me for a man who is neither
haughty nor peeviſh, and who can com-
paſſionate

paffionate human frailty? The more you
avoid me, the more I fhall think you guilty.   Do not hearken to your companions,
but let your heart fpeak, and I fhall inftantly fee you.   Mine prompts me never to
abandon you. I will perfecute you becaufe
I love you, and will give you no reft till
we are reconciled.

It is becaufe I am your beft friend that
I feek to find you, at a time when fcarce
any of your relations will hear your name
mentioned.

If you dread my remonftrances, I fhall
fay nothing to you, becaufe I fhall be convinced that you will accufe yourfelf, and
allow me no time to fpeak.   Try at leaft
one vifit; and if that is not agreeable, you
fhall never fee me more.   But I know
your heart—I know my own - and I am
certain, that after one interview you will
have no defire to leave me.

I ought naturally to have a greater
afcendancy over your mind, who have
known you thefe twenty years, than all the
young affociates who furround you, to de-

vour your eftate, and are your friends only to ruin your health and reputation.

If my tears can affect you, I proteft to you that they flow at this inftant, and from the moft precious motives in the world—Religion and Friendfhip. Come and dry them up ; it will prove to me that you ftill remember your father, and are fenfible to the diftrefs of a friend.

ROME, 1ft Feb. 1750.

LETTER XXI.

TO THE ABBE NICOLINI.

SIR,

THE picture of infidelity you have drawn alarms, without aftonifhing, me.——Befides its being foretold, even to the leaft *iota*, in the Holy Scriptures, the mind is capable of going aftray the greateft lengths, when the heart is once corrupted. From a defire that there fhould be no God to punifh crimes, the wicked conclude that he doth not exift— *Dixit im-pius*

pius in corde suo, Non eft Deus. Deifm leads imperceptibly to Atheifm—we have no compafs, when we have no Religion; it is the only prop by which we can be reafonably fupported.

Notwithftanding the dreadful confequences of this new philofophy, I am of opinion that we ought not to exafperate thofe who profefs it. There are people unconvinced who deferve to be pitied, becaufe, after all, faith is a gift from God. Jefus Chrift, who thundered at the Pharifees, faid nothing to the Sadducees. Unbelievers will be much eafier led back by gentlenefs than by feverity. They affect a haughtinefs to thofe who wound them keenly; and the more fo, becaufe they are anfwered frequently with much worfe reafoning than is found even in their own difcourfes and writings. The moft petty Ecclefiaftic eagerly fets about attacking them without reflecting, that though his zeal is laudable, his underftanding by no means keeping pace with it, he may do more harm than good.

G 5   Converts

Converts are not made either by declamation or invective. Examples, reason, and moderation are requisite, and we should begin by allowing, that Religion has indeed mysteries which are incomprehensible, and which cannot all be explained. There is a chain reaching from heaven to earth, and unless we keep hold of the links, we shall never confute infidelity. Vague declamation is not reasoning, to contend with able men in the arts of sophistry, knowledge, method, and precision are wanted.

When I meet with people who have the prejudices of this new philosophy, which happens pretty often, I begin by inspiring them with confidence, and speak to them with the greatest candour. They are sensible of this, if they have had only the slightest tincture of education, and that at least lessens their prejudices.

Every impetuous zeal which would bring down fire from Heaven, excites only hatred. The Church has the reputation of being of a persecuting spirit, in the eyes of unbelievers, from many of its ministers
showing

showing a too ardent zeal. A good cause supports itself—so that Religion needs only to produce its proofs, its traditions, its works, and its gentleness, to be respected. Christianity of itself overthrows every sect which may be inclined to schism, or which breathes a spirit of animosity.

I frequently meet with people who really detest the whole body of the Clergy, and those are the people whom principally I endeavour to be well with. If I had leisure and abilities to combat the new philosophy, I have the presumption to believe that no Philosopher would complain of me. I would lay down principles which could not be denied; and when I met in my way with those too celebrated men who profess infidelity, I would show them with the greatest candour, that they have not taken the Holy Scriptures in their true sense, or that they have no good reasons for their denying their authenticity.

I am sensible I should not convert them, since it is God alone who enlighteneth the understanding, and changeth the heart: but at least they would not be so apt to

inveigh

inveigh againſt the defenders of Religion. We muſt endeavour to gain ſomething, if we cannot gain all.

If God bears with unbelievers, we ought to bear with them, ſince **they** make a part of **his** plan; and by them Religion appears ſtronger, and the faith of the righteous is exerciſed.

It **is not at** all ſuppriſing that ages of ſuperſtition ſhould lead the way to an age of infidelity—but theſe are tempeſts which paſs over, and only ſhow the face of Heaven more pure and **ſerene.**

The more that unbelievers increaſe, the more ought the Miniſters of the Goſpel to be attentive to render Religion reſpectable by their love of ſtudy, and the purity of their morals. I have here thrown together **a** number of things which you knew before.—My pen leads me on infenſibly— it is a fault with which I frequently reproach it, but it is incorrigible. I beg your pardon for it, in favour **of** my intention, and in conſideration of the pleaſure I have in aſſuring you of the reſpectful and ſincere attachment with which I am, &c.

It

It is some time since I had any accounts of M. Cerati. I am the more uneasy, because he should have answered me upon an affair of consequence.

ROME, 28th Feb, 1750.

LETTER XXII.

TO CARDINAL CRESCENCI.

MOST EMINENT,

YOU have solved the case of conscience as it ought to be, conformably with the opinion of the wisest Doctors and particularly according to the sentiments of St. Thomas, whose suffrage is of the greatest weight.

The Holy Office hath not condemned the men his Eminency speaks to me of, as really having commerce with the Devil, but for abusing the most holy words of the service of the Mass and the Psalms, in order to carry on their extravagant operations. It is known that sorcerers now-a-days are not supernatural agents, and that a be-a belief of Necromancy (though according to the Scripture the Devil is a real being) is almoſt always the effeſt of ſuperſtition, or the work of a troubled brain.

I kiſs your hands with the profoundeſt reſpeſt, in expeſtation of the moment when we ſhall kiſs your feet, if the prophecy attributed to St. Philip of Neri take place, as it is commonly reported.

Fr. L. Ganganelli.

Rome, 1ſt March, 1750.

LETTER XXIII.

TO A GENTLEMAN OF RAVENNA.

SIR,

I COULD never have ſuſpeſted that you would apply to an obſcure Monk, like me, to decide a family-diſpute. There are a great number of learned Lawyers here, who can give you a proper opinion.

Beſides my incapacity in this affair, I am not fond of giving advice in ſecular matters.

ters. I remember that St. Paul prohibits every Minifter of the Lord from interfering in temporals. A man who is dead to the world, fhould not intermeddle in the affairs of it. Every Religious Society that neglects this maxim, will fink into oblivion fooner or later—as every Monk who intrudes into families to know their fecrets, to regulate marriages and teftaments, is equally contemptible and dangerous.

We have too many duties of our own, to have leifure to bufy ourfelves in other people's affairs ; and at prefent we fhould be detefted, if we dared to attempt it. We made noife enough formerly, by ftriving only to preferve the ufe or property of our own rights ; let us not meddle now-a-days with the inheritances of the world. St. Francis, who preached up difintereftednefs and poverty, would anathematife us, if he faw us attempting to undertake the province of fecular affairs.

All that I ought, or can do, is to exhort you to peace and concord, and not to fhow a criminal avidity for the things of this life, which paffeth away, and leaves us nothing

thing but our works. Let us endeavour to improve them, that we may not appear before God empty-handed.

ROME, 3d March, 1750.

LETTER XXIV.

TO CARDINAL QUIRINI.

MOST EMINENT,

I LOVE to fee a Library in your Eminency's poffeffion—it is certain that it will not be covered with duft, nor remain unemployed. By the manner in which you fpeak to me of it, and the difcernment I know you poffefs, it will be worth the admiration of the curious. I fhall always remember the having paffed a day with your Eminency, Cardinal Paffionei, and a number of other Literati—it will be the faireft and the moft precious epoch of my life. I then faw the moft learned men in Europe, and I drank at the fource from the two fineft intellectual rivers in the world. There were agitated the moft important queftions, without affectation, obftinacy,

or

or pride. Only the half-learned and half-wife make themfelves noted by their obftinacy and vanity; but what ftruck me moft was, that Genius, which does not always accompany learning, feemed there to fpring from the womb of Science, like lightening from Heaven.

As the candour of thefe two great men muft captivate every liberal mind, I fhould have **been** delighted to be witnefs of an interview between them and fome of our modern Philofophers. Some time ago I reminded Cardinal Paffionei of this anecdote; and his memory, which is very great, and always ready, enabled him to repeat fuccinctly every thing that was then faid.

I earneftly wifh, my Lord, to be able to accompany you to Mount Caffino. You muft appear radiant there, like Mofes upon mount Sinai — it is your centre, and the cradle in which you have acquired that fuperior knowledge, which renders you the worthy fucceffor of fo many illuftrious men as have fprung from thence.

It appears to me, my Lord, if I dare make that confeffion to you, that your laft
                                        letter

letter to the Proteftant Clergy is a little too dry. Your Eminency knows better than I do, how neceffary it is to ufe the moft engaging manner in order to gain over Profelytes. Nothing can be added to the profound refpect with which I am, &c.

LETTER XXV.

TO R. P. ORSI, A DOMINICAN, BUT SINCE BECOME CARDINAL.

MY REV. FATHER,

I HAVE been twice to call upon you, without having the happinefs to find you, although you are fo fedentary a Reclufe. I wanted to thank you for the book you fent me. I congratulate Italy on the happy production with which you have enriched it. M. Fleury had occafion for a writer to fill up the chafms in his hiftory; for it muft be confeffed, notwithftanding the refpect which I have for his memory, that he has flightly touched a number of very important facts. Perhaps he was not
poffeffed

poffeffed of fufficient memoirs for fome articles : we fhould weigh the charge well, before we condemn fo great a man.

In the mean time, I cannot pardon his having faid almoft nothing of the Church of Ravenna, fo celebrated in the annals of Italy by a multitude of incidents relative to its Exarchs. Sometimes a follicitude for being too concife is dangerous ; it makes us only give fketches when we ought to prefent finifhed pieces.

We reproach M. Fleury with being too zealous for the liberties of the Gallican Church ; and the French will accufe you, my Reverend Father, of fupporting the ultramontane opinions too warmly.

See then how difficult it is for a writer to pleafe every Government ; but fenfible men give up the French and Romans their different pretenfions, if the Faith be not affected.   Every country has its opinion, as every individual his whim.

I wifh that your labours may meet with a brilliant recompence, not for your glory, but the glory of the Church ; you have no occafion for the purple to render you illuftrious.

trious. As for me, I think myself the moſt honoured of men, when you receive with cordiality the ſincere and reſpectful ſentiments with which I am irrevocably, &c.

ROME, 11th of June, 1750.

LETTER XXVI.

TO A PRELATE.

MY LORD,

I HAVE written ſo much, that my hand ought to be tired; but it has more vigour than ever, while it is employed in expreſſing the ſentiments with which you inſpire me.

Notwithſtanding my occupations, I have done all that you preſcribed. I have ſeen the perſon you mentioned—I have got the better of her reſiſtance.—She will take care of the little orphan, as you deſire. Other peoples' misfortunes render me ſingularly eloquent; then my heart, ſoul, and mind, ſpeak at once.

The

The Monks are reproached with being felfifh; were that the cafe, I fhould never have been one——but it is a calumny which I will not attempt to refute. The meanneffes of human nature are to be found in Cloifters, only becaufe they are inhabited by men—yet there are **men** every-where. This does not prevent our feeing a great many virtues in a Monaftery. I proteft to you, I am afhamed of myfelf, when I obferve fome venerable perfonages with whom I live, inceffantly employed in doing good offices, from morning till night. The world judges of Communities only from fome fcandals which unfortunately blaze abroad, without attending to the talents and the virtues which are perpetuated there.

The monaftick life would be very honourable, if it was duely honoured : and men powerful both in words and in works would never be wanting in it. Emulation is abfolutely neceffary in a Cloifter, in order to preferve a love of ftudy; as ambition is its fcandal and ruin. There **is no** greater monfter in Church or State than

than an hypocritical ambitious clergyman, who, profeffing to be humble, is puffed up with pride—a man who, wearing an out-fide of poverty, feeks only to enrich him-felf—a falfe devotee, who announces him-felf the fervant of God, yet is only the flave of his own paffions.

When I think that there are Monks, who embrace their own deftruction to ob-tain a wretched fuperiority of rank or pre-ferment, fubject to a thoufand vexations, and a thoufand inconveniencies, I cannot define man ; and, I fay, that he damns himfelf for a very little matter.

O my dear folitude ! my books and my labours ! what vexation would it give me, were I obliged to give you up, to mix in the tumult of bufinefs and honours ! Even the title of Majefty would not make amends to a man for the liberty he lofes, when he becomes a King.

I was taught to believe from my earlieft days, that the honour of having an im-mortal foul is the greateft poffible glory ; and happily I have retained the leffon.

I would

I would not fay this to all the world, for there are very few capable of comprehending it; but I am underftood by you who have a relifh for the ineftimable pleafures of exifting and thinking. I embrace you with all my heart, and am without referve

Your friend and fervant.

LETTER XXVII.

TO MONSIGNOR HENRIQUEZ;

My Lord,

YOU deign to confult me, while I ftand more in need of your advice. Your underftanding and piety are known ; and it is univerfally allowed that you are the beft guide, and the moft learned Doctor.

However, to fhow my obedience, I muft fay that the depofit ought to be fent to *Peter*, although it was deftined for him by *John*, folely on account of his attach-

5   ment,

ment to the Roman Catholic Religion, and though he has unfortunately changed his faith.

It is only neceffary to acquaint him with the intention of his benefactor, when he made that bequeft in his favour. But I do not think that the perfon charged with the depofit, can withold it from him becaufe he has changed his Religion.

You fay, my Lord, that there are people who maintain that it may be made a gift to fome Monaftery; but tho' a Monk, I dare affert, that it would be an unjuft appropriation—in the firft place, becaufe it fhould be given to him to whom it was bequeathed: fecondly, becaufe in the partition of property, families fhould always have the preference; thirdly and laftly, becaufe the poor, who have no means of fubftance, ought chiefly to be fupported.

Providence is the refource of Communities, and their dependence ought to be rather upon That, than on human means. All Religious Orders are eftimable only as they imitate Jefus Chrift; but we too often have fome worldly views for the fupport

of

of Monasteries, without reflecting that the true Christian has no permanent habitation in this world, and that nothing happens but as it pleaseth God.

Nevertheless I submit my judegment to your's, never having any obstinate attachment to my own opinions. I display them conformably to the dictates of my conscience, and I take every possible precaution to be informed; for there is no evil we are not capable of, even while we have the best intentions, if we follow no other guide than an ignorant devotion.

I have the honour to be, &c.

LETTER XXVIII.

TO THE ABBESS OF A MONASTERY.

MY MOST REV. MOTHER,

FROM the narrative which you have sent me, it appears that you cannot conveniently take vigorous measures. If your Nuns are become dissipated, and they lead you as they please, there is an end of all rule. Diffipation, and efpecially the Parlour, are the ruin of all Convents of Nuns. Recollection and application only can preferve order in the different Communities. The Cloifter is an infupportable yoke, while a profpect is open from thence into the world, and the more frequent opportunities of converfation the Nuns enjoy, the more they muft become difgufted with their condition.

I fuppofe that you frequently affemble your Community, and, like a good mother who loves her children, lay before them the effufions of your heart, upon the neceffity of fulfilling their duties. I would then have you endeavour to perfuade them, that your confcience reproaches you for your ill-placed lenity : and that if you are obliged to appear more fevere, it is becaufe your falvation is at ftake.

When your Nuns find that you are not governed by any harfhnefs of temper, but by a dread of failing in your duty to God, they will hearken to you with refpect, or will be of the number of the foolifh Virgins who have neither oil nor light in their

lamps

lamps to go and meet the Bridegroom. This would be the moſt affecting misfortune that could happen; and then, when you have exhauſted every reſource which prudence and charity dictate, you muſt employ the lawful authority of a Superior to reform them.

But, my Reverend **Mother, I** preſume that you will not have occaſion to come to this extremity. They will murmur againſt you for ſome time; but the anger of Nuns paſſeth like a ſhower, provided there **be** no cabals nor parties; but then God only can diſpel them.

It is difficult to reſiſt a Superior, who prays, begs, and humbles herſelf: who employs tears, **rather** than reproaches, to affect and perſuade. Ah! I wiſh **to** God that **this was the** ordinary language of all Abbeſſes! But, alas! there are too many, who, intoxicated with chimerical rank, without merit, **but** poſſeſſing a large ſhare of caprice and haughtineſs, live apart from their Nuns, and paſs much of their time at their toilets, and in the parlour. Theſe are fooliſh Virgins (yet perhaps they do

H 2

not

not deferve that name) who are the ruin and fcandal of Communities, and abide in them only like wafps in a hive, to devour the honey and to breed confufion.

In afking my advice, Madam, you have impofed upon me a fevere tafk, for I have no talent for directing, Nuns efpecially. I think like our Father St. Francis, pardon my fincerity, who faid, *that God has debarred us from having wives, that we may be infpired with a defire of being religious; but I am afraid the Devil has given us fifters to torment us.* He knew how difficult it is to direct Nuns, although there are fome among them exceedingly docile, and of excellent underftandings—there is not even a fingle Community which does not contain fome worthy of the higheft encomiums.

After all this, Madam, I muft beg of you not to addrefs me again upon this fubject; and the rather, becaufe I have not time to anfwer you, and that I can fay nothing better than what your Rules tell you. Talk but little with your Directors, and a great deal with God, and peace will
flourifh

flourifh again in your Abbey. I wifh it
on your own account, and for the honour
of Religion, being with all poffible re-
fpeꜹ, &c.

ROME, 10th Nov, 1750.

LETTER XXIX.

TO THE ABBE LAMI, PERIODICAL WRITER
AT FLORENCE.

I ALWAYS read your writings with
pleafure, my dear Abbé, but I wifh
you would always give the reafons of your
cenfures. Inftead of faying, for example,
that the ftyle of fuch a work is incorreꜹ ; that
there are trifles which disfigure the beauty of
the book ; you fhould plainly prove the
charge. Rules have always need of examples.

How would you have an author correꜹ
himfelf, and the Publick adopt your manner of judging, if you only cenfure vague-
ly, and do not point out the place where
the writer has forgot himfelf?

H 3   There.

There is hardly any book of which it may not be faid, that it contains fome care-lefs or affected expreffions. When you fpeak in general, it gives room to believe that you have only glanced your eye over the work of which you are giving an account, and that you are in hafte to get rid of the trouble.

Another omiffion is, your not fhowing the beft parts of the work. The good tafte of the Journalift (Reviewer) requires that he fhould be attentive to this. If a work is not worth the trouble of reading, it is better not to announce it at all, than to rail at the Writer. It is illiberal to abufe a work merely to make the Publick merry at the expence of the Author.

It were to be wifhed that Rome would adopt the practice of Paris, and that we had feveral periodical fheets appear fuc-ceffively. We have only a miferable *Diario* (Journal) a farrago of uninftructive infi-pidity. Where letters are cultivated, the duty of an enlightened Reviewer is both neceffary and honourable. Nobody knows better than I do, what a country owes to a

Writer

Writer who ties himfelf down to give an analyfis of the books that are printed every week, or every month, and thus to make known the genius of the nation. It is the leaft expenfive, and the moft compendious method of extending knowledge, and of teaching to judge foundly.

I fhould have no idea of the ftate of li-terature in France, if it were not for the French Journals, which my friends are fo obliging as to fend me. When they are fevere without fatire, exact without trifling, juft and impartial, they difcharge their duty to the fatisfaction of the Publick. Mine is complete, every time that I can renew to you the fentiments of efteem and affection with which

I am, &c.

LETTER XXX.

TO COUNT ***.

IT is incredible, my deareſt friend, how
much your three viſits have comforted
my ſoul—the tears you ſhed in my prefence, the confeſſion you made to me, while
you joined your cheek to mine, preſſed my
hand, and proteſted that you would never
forget the anxiety with which I endeavoured to find you out ; the affecting manner
in which you promiſed me to amend your
paſt life, and endeavour ſeriouſly to re-
enter into favour with God, can never be
effaced from my memory, nor from my
heart. I always ſaid to myſelf, " He hath
" had a Chriſtian education — he will return
" to his duty—I ſhall ſee him again ; his
" wanderings are but a ſtorm, which will
" diſperſe." God be praiſed, the calm is
returned !—It is not to me, but to him
alone, that you ſhould be thankful.

Since you wiſh that I ſhould lay down a
plan to guide you, I ſhall ſimply trace out
ſuch a one as my weak underſtanding,

but

but ſtrong friendſhip inſpires—it ſhall be
ſhort. The Commandments of God, thoſe
firſt and ſublime laws, from whence all
others are derived, may be reduced to a
few words. Precepts that are clear and
founded upon reaſon, as well as happineſs,
have no need of commentary or diſſer-
tation.

Read every morning the parable of the
Prodigal Son—repeat the Pſalm *Miſerere,*
with an humble and contrite heart—That
may ſerve for prayer. Read ſome religious
books in the courſe of the day, not like
a ſlave to finiſh his taſk, but as a child of
God who returns to his Father, and hopes
every thing from his mercy: and that it
may not diſguſt you, your reading need
not be long. Acquire the habit of going
to Maſs as often as you can, but never
fail on Sundays and Feſtivals—aſſiſt there
like a ſuppliant who beggeth pardon, with
hopes to obtain it.

Make it a duty to ſcatter ſome charities
every day into the boſoms of the poor,
that you may repair the wrongs you have
done them, in ſquandering on criminal

H 5   pleaſures

pleasures and superfluities what was due to them. Renounce those companions who have estranged you from God, from yourself, and from your true friends; and form such new connections as honour, decency, and Religion, may avow. It is easy to dismiss debauched associates, without affronting them. Speak openly to them of the plan of life you mean to pursue; propose to them to follow it; talk to them only of regretting the past, and forming good resolutions for the future, and they will soon disappear; or, if they return, it will be a proof that they have altered their conduct; and then, instead of shunning them, receive them with more pleasure than ever.

Walk often, lest retirement should make you grow melancholy; and provide, if possible, some person ripened by experience, or some virtuous young man, for a companion. Walk alone as seldom as possible, and especially in these beginnings, while your resolutions are not well confirmed. It may happen, that by giving way to vague thoughts you may soon grow tired of yourself;

yourfelf; and again relapfe into your former courfe of life.

Read fome agreeable but inftructive book to entertain you in virtuous chearfulnefs. Melancholy is the wreck of young people who are employed about their converfion—they **are** always drawing a parallel between **the** diffipated life they have led, and the ferious life which is prefcribed them; and they end with returning to their former courfes.

Take an exact account of your debts **and** your income, and by your œconomy you will find wherewith to pay your creditors. A man is always rich, when he is in the habit **of** depriving himfelf of indulgences; as he **is** always poor while he refufes himfelf nothing.

You fhould fettle an annuity for **life** upon the **woman** you have feduced, that want **may not oblige** her to continue an irregular life; **but** upon condition that fhe goes **to a** diftance from **you**—announce your intentions in writing, begging pardon for having feduced her, **and** conjuring her to forget the crea-

H 6 ture,

ture, that she may be more attached to her Creator.

When opportunities offer of enjoying a little society, do **not** refuse them, because you may be properly employed **there**; and because you will be secured **from** the raillery of the world, which is fond of turning piety into ridicule.

Dress like the rest of the world, according **to** your rank in life, without being either **too** foppish **or too** neglient. True Religion shuns extremes; **it is** only when counterfeited, that men affect **a** slovenly dress, a declining head, an austere **countenance, and** a whining tone.

Dismiss **the** servants who **were** accomplices in your intrigues, and sharers in your guilt; although, after having exposed them **to** scandal, it would be proper to set them a good example, yet it is to be dreaded, from their knowledge of your weakness, that they might lay snares to lead you back into **the** road of perdition. You are still young enough to secure your heart with proper guards and fences.

4

With

With your new domesticks, whose abilities and fidelity have been properly recommended to you, you should live as a master who knows the duties of humanity; as a christian who knows that we are all equal in the sight of God, notwithstanding the inequality of conditions—you will set them none but good examples; watch over their manners, without either being a tyrant or a spy; and attach them to you by your gentleness and your beneficence. Nothing can be so flattering as to render those happy who live with us.

I exhort you to visit the Chapel in the inside of the Chartreux, which was built by the order of Cardinal Cibo, whose memory I respect. Rather than mix his ashes with those of his illustrious progenitors, which rest in superb monuments, he would be interred in the midst of his domesticks, whose epitaphs he made; contenting himself only with these words, so expressive of humility; *Hic jacet Cibo, vermis immundus* *.

This tomb is absolutely hidden from the sight of men; but God, to whom all things

* Here lies Cibo, an unclean worm.

things are known, will make it manifeft at the laft day, which will be a fad reproach to thofe proud men who are vain even in their coffins.

You muft think of taking fome charge upon you which will give you employment. We always do amifs when we do nothing. Examine your underftanding, confult your tafte, afk your heart : but above all, addrefs yourfelf to God, that you may know what is fit for you, whether civil or military. The life of an Ecclefiaftick is by no means proper for you. We ought not to carry into the Sanctuary the remains of a heart ftained by commerce with the world, unlefs the will of God is manifefted in an extraordinary manner; which is very rare, and the example is much more to be admired than imitated.

Your friends will think next of marrying you, and it is my advice not to defer it too long. Marriage, when made with purity of heart, preferves young people from a multitude of dangers; but do not reckon upon my choofing a wife for you. From the moment I embraced my profeffion,

fion, I promifed to God that I would never meddle in marriages or teftaments. A Monk is a man buried, who ought not to fhow any figns of life, but for things purely fpiritual, becaufe the foul never dies.

Your relation, with whom I have happily reconciled you, is a man of fenfe, honefty, and integrity, and in a fituation to marry you properly. Religion and reafon ought to be confulted more than inclination, in an eftablifhment that is to laft for life. We rarely fee marriages happy, which have no other motive than love. That paffion does wonders in poetry and romance, but in real life produces no good effect.

I do not fpeak to you of your expences, nor of your table. With fuch principles as I lay down, they muft be moderate. Frequently invite fome virtuous friend to dinner. I do not like to fee you alone, and I reccommend to you to be fo as little as poffible, except when you are at your prayers or reading—*It is not good for man to be alone*, faith the Scripture.

Vifit

Vifit your eftate only now and then. If you take up your refidence in the country at this time, you will bury your good refolutions, as well as your education. Rural focieties lead only to diffipation ; and however little they are frequented, the effect is, that you forget what you knew, and become ruftic, illiterate, and clownifh. Hunting, love, and wine, too often become the paftimes of men who live conftantly in the country. Towns polifh the manners, adorn the mind, and prevent the foul from gathering ruft. Do not be fcrupuloufly exact about the hour of rifing or going to bed. Order is neceffary in all ranks, but conftraint and formality too often produces narrow-mindednefs.

If you look upon Religion in the great, as it ought to be viewed, you will not find in it the trifling of puerile devotion. Never open thofe myftical or apocryphal books, which, under pretence of nourifhing piety, amufe the foul with infignificant ceremonies, leaving the mind without light, and the heart without compunction. *True Devotion*, written by the celebrated Muratori,

Muratori, will preferve you from all the dangers of a miftaken credulity. I advife you to read that work again and again ; and you will profit by it.

Do not receive indifcriminate counfels ; for in the difeafes of the foul, as in thofe of the body, every one offers his advice. Avoid the hypocrite as well as the diffi-pated ; both the one and the other will hinder you from arriving at the point we propofe. I will not look upon you as a convert, 'till you have been a long time proved. It is not eafy to pafs from liber-tinifm to the practice of virtue—it is for that reafon that I recommend, for your Director, the good Francifcan, who was your Father's friend, and is mine. He is an excellent guide in fpirituals ; and if he keeps you fome time before you are admit-ted to the participation of the holy myfte-ries, it is becaufe he would be affured, with reafon, that you are changed, and follow the conftant practice of the Church. Do not be afraid of his feverity—he will join the tendernefs of a father to the fteadinefs of a wife Director—he will not opprefs

you

you with attentions to externals, as lefs knowing Confeffors generally do. If you have finned through pride, he will point out to you the means of humbling your-felf——if through fenfuality, he will prefcribe remedies to mortify you; think-ing, with reafon, that the wounds of the foul are not to be healed by a hafty repeti-tion of prayers, but by labouring to re-form the heart. The generality of finners, for want of this method, pafs their lives in offending God, and then confeffing their fins.

Above all things, let there be no excefs in your piety; take no violent courfes; they will be the means of your relapfing.

Behold, my dear fon, my deareft friend, what I thought it my duty to fketch out for you. I could not ufe more tendernefs, if you were my own. You will make me die with grief, if the refolutions you fo lately entered into, in my prefence, fhould vanifh. What encourages me is, that you are a man of truth, that you have a regard for me, and are fully convinced that I fin-cerely wifh you well; and in the laft place
that

that you have found a diforderly life to be an affemblage of vexation, torment, and remorfe.

Hearken to the voice of a Father crying to you from the bottom of the tomb, that there is no happinefs in this world but for the friends of God, and charging you to keep the promife you formerly made to him, of living, with the help of Heaven, the life of a good Chriftian.

I am a great deal more attached to you than to myfelf.

CONVENT of the HOLY APOSTLES,
    20 Nov, 1750.

P. S. I fhall certainly reconcile you to all your family, except perhaps the Marchionefs of R***, who is too much a devotee ever to pardon you. I expect you to drink chocolate on Saturday, when I fhall communicate a letter to you from poor Sardi, an old fervant of your mother, who is really in want. You do not require much time to come from Viterbo to Rome, efpecially if you have horfes *which* can go *a-foot*.

L E T-

LETTER XXXI.

TO PRINCE SAN SEVERO, A NEAPOLITAN.

My Lord,

I BEG to present my most humble thanks to you for the great civilities you show-ed Mr. Wesler, upon the recommendation of so inconsiderable a man as I am, who do not rank either with the great or the learned. He is exceedingly vain of so flat-tering a reception. He talks with enthu-siasm of all your schemes for the promo-tion of Natural Philosophy, and the ho-nour of Philosophers. There are always new discoveries to be made, equally useful and curious.

Naples is the most proper town in the world to exercise the genius of the learned. It presents on all hands phenomena of eve-ry kind, which engage the attention. Its mountains, its caverns, its stones, its wa-ters, and, if we may use the expression, the fire with which it is penetrated, are so many objects to be examined.

I am

I am not at all furprifed, that the King himfelf is flattered with your labours and your fuccefs. Every Monarch who knows his own glory, knows how much the credit of the learned is reflected back upon him, when he protects them. If thofe Geniufes, who are capable of important undertakings, were encouraged among us, Italy would fee great men of every kind once more fpring up from her bofom. The feeds of Talents ftill remain—they want only to be cherifhed, to flourifh with magnificence.

But the Artifts now begin to lofe that creative genius which worked wonders. Their beft pictures and beft ftatues are only like copies : we may fay, that they force the pencil to work in fpite of itfelf. There is a hardnefs in the drawing, inftead of that fweet foftnefs which is admired in our firft Painters ; and we abfolutely want that expreffion which is the foul of Painting.

We are more rich in Writers. We have ftill fome, who for enegy of ftile, and beauty of images, may be placed by the

fide

fide of the Ancients; fuch as the Abbé *Buona-Fede*, of the Order of Celeftines.

This is an obligation which we owe to our language. By its charms we are engaged to the culture of Letters, as every man is engaged by your talents to tell you, that there is nothing more flattering than to be able to affure you of the refpect and admiration with which, &c.

ROME, 17th of January, 1750.

LETTER XXXII.

TO ONE OF HIS FRIENDS, A FRIAR, APPOINTED PROVINCIAL.

DIGNITIES affect me fo little, that I have not courage to pay my compliments to thofe who are invefted with them. They are an additional fervitude which muft be added to human mifery ; and the more to be dreaded, as they expofe us to pride. Man is fo wretchedly filly as to deck himfelf with trifling honours, which are mere outfide fhow, and forget an immortal foul to feed upon chimerical prerogatives,

which

which laft only a few days. Even in the Cloifter, where all ought to be difintereft-ednefs, felf-denial, and humility, we are as vain of fome preferments, as if we had the command of kingdoms.

I make thefe reflections the more willingly to you, becaufe your turn of mind fets you above all honours, and you have only acquired authority to confer happinefs. I am convinced that you will perfectly temper feverity with gentlenefs; that a cloud will never be feen on your countenance, nor unevennefs in your temper; that you will always be a brother to thofe over whom you are become Superior; that you will endeavour to prefer them according to their inclination and abilities; and that you will employ no fpies, except to difcover the merit of thofe who are too modeft to make a fhow of it.

Thus you will do yourfelf honour by the manner in which you will difcharge your duty, and every one muft defire to fee and detain you; while there are fome Provincials, whofe vifits are dreaded like a tempeft. Above all things, take care, my

dear

dear friend, of the old men and the young people, that the former may be supported, and the latter encouraged as they ought to be. These are extremes which appear very **distant,** yet approach very near, since every young man grows older every instant. **Ob-**serve moderation in all your proceedings, and think it much better to yield to an excess of mildness, than to give way to too great severity.

Speak nobly of Religion, but let it be well-timed ; for people avoid those who are perpetually preaching. Jesus Christ did not make long discourses to his disciples, but what he said to them *is the spirit and the life.* Words have most force, when they are short and pointed. Let there be no affectation in your manner ; there are people who imagine that every thing ought to be formal about men in power ; but these are little minds.

I will not mention duplicity, unfortunately too much practised by the Heads of Religious Houses. I flatter myself, from the good opinion I have of your merit, that you will not prefer a complaint against any

one,

one, without having several times warned
him of your intention, or without previ-
ously acquainting him. Be afraid of finding any guilty; and when you meet such,
humble yourself by this reflection, that
man of himself is incapable of doing any
good. Be communicative, for we lose much
of the good-will of those we govern, by
disgusting coldness. In a word, be yourself
what you wished a Provincial to be, when
you was an Inferior.   But we too often exact from others what we ourselves are not
inclined to give. Distinguish faults by the
motives and circumstances; and know, that
though there are some which ought to be
punished, there are others which ought not
to be seen, because every man has his im-
perfections.

Have few confidents; but when you
make any, let it not be by halves; for they
will divine the rest of your secret, and are
not obliged to keep it. Be sure to have no
predilection in favour of one rather than
another, except on account of superior merit. You are then authorised by the example of Christ himself, who testified a

VOL. I.   I   particular

particular affection for St. Peter and St. John.

Finally, pass into the Houses like a beneficent dew, so that they shall regret the time when you leave your office, and say of you, *Transit benefaciendo* *.

Love me as I love you, and look upon this letter as the transcript of my heart.

My compliments to our common friends, especially our respectable old man, whose good advice has been of the greatest utility to me, and to whom my gratitude is immortal.

ROME, 31st Jan. 1751.

LETTER XXXIII.

TO MADAME THE MARCHIONESS R***.

MADAM,

IT is undoubtedly very distressing to your dear relation, M. the Count, that you will not be reconciled to him, notwithstanding his visit, and the humble and affecting letter he has written to you.

Is

* He scattered blessings as he passed.

Is it thus God Almighty deals with *us?*
What will the world think of your piety,
when they fee you fo exafperated as to reject the Prodigal Son? For my part, Madam, who have not your virtue, I flew to
him as foon as I knew that he was gone
aftray, and I hope that God will reward
me for it.

You are always repeating, Madam, that
he has loft a great deal of money, and that
he is a bad man. But what is even the lofs
of gold, that you fhould fo much regret
it? You ought only to be grieved at the
abufe of fo many good qualities as he pof-
feffes; and think, if he is really a bad man,
that he has more need than ever of advice,
and the example of the truely good.

It is having a very bad idea of Religion,
to forfake a young man, becaufe he has
committed fome errors.

Ah! how do you know, Madam, that
this bad man will not next day be accept-
able in the fight of God, while your fervices may by no means pleafe him? For
truely one grain of pride is fufficient to fpoil
the beft actions. The Pharifee who fafted

two

two days in the week, was rejected; and the Publican who humbled himſelf was juſtified.

Charity, with regard to all men, and always charity! this I ſhall never ceaſe to repeat, as perfectly agreeable to the morals taught in every Chriſtian ſchool, and from all pulpits.

If the mercy of God depended upon certain devotees, ſinners would be much to be pitied:—falſe devotion knows nothing but an exterminating zeal; while God, full of patience, gentleneſs, and forbearance, waits the amendment of all thoſe who have gone aſtray.

Even the blood of Chriſt implores your forgiveneſs; and it is not having a proper reſpect for him, to refuſe your dear relation admittance into your houſe. How do you know, Madam, but that his ſalvation depended upon thoſe very faults of which he now repenteth? God frequently permits great diſorders, to awaken men out of a lethargy. You are not ignorant that there is more joy in Heaven over *one ſinner that repenteth, than over ninety and nine juſt*

3   *perſons*

perfons that need no repentance. Befides, will you continue your refentment while the Angels rejoice ? That would be a fhocking fort of piety, indeed !

I tremble for every devotee who behaves with fuch rigidity ; for God Almighty himfelf affures us, that he will treat us as we have treated others. Be fo good as to read the Epiftle of St. Paul to Philemon, on the fubject of Onefimus, and there you will know, Madam, whether you ought to pardon.

It is not for us to decide, whether the heart of a man who appears to have entered ferioufly into himfelf is truely changed. Befides, as God alone can know the truth, we ought to prefume that he has reformed. Would you think it very juft in your neighbours, who are the witneffes of your good works, if they fuppofed that you acted only from pride ? Let us leave to the Searcher of all hearts to pronounce what are the motives of our actions.—The brother of the Prodigal Son is condemned in the eyes of Religion and Humanity, for not being properly affected at his return.

I 3

If

If I was your Ghoſtly Father, although
the direction of conſciences is neither ana-
logous to my labours, nor agreeable to my
inclination, in order to appeaſe your anger,
I would enjoin you to write to him who is
ſo hateful in your ſight—to ſee him often,
and even on the condition of forgetting
what is paſt.

If our piety is to be regulated by whim,
virtue is only a phantom; and I certainly
preſume, that your's has charity for its
foundation; for I never judge unfavour-
ably of my neighbour.

If my letter, contrary to my intention,
appears a little ſevere, I beg you will think
I ſpeak in ſuch a manner, leſs on your relation's account, than your own; for your
ſalvation depends upon it. Will you not
pardon him, when you have reaſon to preſume that God Almighty hath pardoned
him? I cannot think it.

I have the honour to be, with reſpect,
&c.

Rome, 5th Feb. 175'.

L E T-

LETTER XXXIV.

TO THE CHEVALIER DE CABANE.

SIR,

YOU perfevere, then, in your intention to bury yourfelf at La Trappe,
and to put it out of my power to addrefs
you in future, but by writing your epi-
taph? Since it is your determination, I
will not perfift in oppofing you, becaufe
you have been long tried, and are not of
an age to take any inconfiderate ftep.

The world will laugh at you, but pray
what does it not laugh at? I know no perfon, no work, no proceeding of any kind,
nor even a virtue, without its cenfures.
This fhould be a confolation to the Religious Orders for the hatred the world bears
them, and the contempt with which they
are fpoken of.

Too great encomiums were made upon
them when they were firft inftituted, and
fome counterpoife was neceffary to pre-

I 4 ferve

ferve their humility. The Founders had the beft intentions in forming the different inftitutions in the bofom of the church; and even the habits which they gave their Difciples, though reckoned by the world fantaftical, prove their wifdom and their piety. They thought thefe habits a means of preventing the Religious from mixing with the Seculars, and of excluding them from profane affemblies. It was natural for men who embraced a kind of life entirely different from the cuftoms of the world, to wear particular habits.

Thus, then, they are juftified upon that head. How eafy would it be to apologife for the reft, if I was not of the profeffion myfelf! Read their rules, examine their cuftoms, and it is impoffible not to acknowledge, that all which is recommended, and all that is obferved in the Cloifters, leads to the Creator.

If they have degenerated fince their firft inftitution, it is becaufe man is naturally weak, and at the end of a certain time the greateft fervour muft relax. But nothing
fcandalous

fcandalous ever became a rule among the
Religious Orders; there are fome in every
Houfe who declare againft all kinds of
irregularities and exceffes.

They who rail continually againft the
Monks, who wifh to deprive them of their
poffeffions, and to banifh them from every
State, are certainly ignorant of their being
invited into the different kingdoms by the
Kings themfelves, who endowed them, and
loaded them with benefactions. They muft
be ignorant, if the foundations of Kings
are not facred, there is no longer any thing
in the world that fhould be fpared; and
that in fhort, the Monks, againft whom
they fo bitterly inveigh, have gained by the
fweat of their brows, by their watchings,
and by their labours, the bread which
nourifheth them.

Their pretended rapacioufnefs is only
calumny. The Benedictines acquired their
property by cultivating the country and
the Lord's vineyard, at a time when Ignorance and Corruption made the greateft
devaftation. The firft difciples of St. Do-

minick, of St. Francis d'Affifi, and St. Francis de Paul, afked nothing from Kings, while they had their moft perfect confidence, and could obtain every thing; as may be proved by their indigence.

I know there are monafteries which by their mifconduct have often made a reformation neceffary; but neither the Monaftic rules nor the Founders deferve to be blamed. A man who lives in a Cloifter according to its rules, cannot but excite the efteem, and deferve the attachment of all good men. For what is a true Monk but a citizen of Heaven, who values not this world, who makes a facrifice of his will and his fenfes to God himfelf, in the perfon of his Superior, and who continually wifheth for the coming of the Lord— who inftructs and edifies for the good of his neighbour—who fhows in a chearful countenance the joys of a good confcience, and the charms of virtue— who prays, who labours, who ftudies for himfelf, and for his brethren—who lays himfelf at the feet of the whole world by his humility, but is exalted above all men

by

by the fublimity of his hopes. and his defires—who poffeffeth nothing but a foul
in peace—who wifheth for nothing but
Heaven—who liveth only to die, and dieth
to live again to all eternity?

Behold what you are to be, my deareft
Sir! I do not mention the Rules of your
Order, fince by the obfervance of them
you will have no further commerce with
mankind; which is the only thing that
gives me pain, becaufe I love that we
fhould be ufeful to our neighbour.

Time, which is an oppreffive load to the
generality of men, will be no burthen to
you. Every minute will feem a ftep towards Heaven; and night itfelf will be to
you as light as day, from the commerce
you will hold with God. *Et nox ficut dies
illuminabitur.*

You will not hear the bell which calls
you to fervice, only as a bell, but as the
voice of God—you will not obey the
Abbé fimply as a man, but as one who
holds the place of Jefus Chrift, and who
will fpeak to you in his name—you will
not look upon penance as a flavery which

I 6   muft

muft not be difpenfed with, but as a holy pleafure which will be your delight.

You will omit none of the fmalleft Rules which fubdue the fpirit, and oppofe the will; for a Monk cannot preferve the fervour of devotion, but by practifing exactly what is recommended as well as what is commanded : thus you will preferve the liberty of the children of God, by doing voluntary, and with pleafure, whatever may be required from you as a duty of obligation.

I fhall be happy to fee you according to your promife, having no greater fatisfaction than to find myfelf with the true fervants of God, efpecially as in thefe days they are extremely rare.

I can add nothing, but that I am, &c.

Rome, 15th March, 1751.

L E T-

LETTER XXXV.

TO THE BISHOP OF SPOLETTO.

My Lord,

WHAT your Lordſhip wrote to me on the ſubject of the relicks of Saints, does honour to your diſcernment and to your Religion. There are two rocks to be ſhunned by all true Catholics—that of believing too much, and that of not believing enough. If we were to give credit to all the ſtories told of the relicks which are ſhown in every country, we muſt frequently ſuppoſe that a Saint had ten heads or ten arms.

This abuſe, which has procured us the name of ſuperſtitious, has happily only taken root among the ignorant. Thank Heaven, it is well known in Italy (and the Clergy repeat it often enough) that there is nothing abſolutely neceſſary but the mediation of Jeſus Chriſt; that of the Saints, as the Council of Trent hath formally declared, being only *good and uſeful*.

The

The relicks of the Blessed deserve all our veneration, as precious remains which will one day be gloriously revived ; but while we honour them, we acknowledge that they have no virtue in themselves, and that it is Jesus Christ, of whom they are in some sort fragments ; and the Holy Ghost, of whom they are the true temples, who communicate to them a heavenly impression capable of working great wonders.

Notwithstanding this, the attention to the worship due to God is but too often taken off by that which is paid to saints. Hence that wise order was given in Rome, never to place relicks upon the altar where the *venerabile* (the holy sacrament) is deposited, lest they should divide the attention of the people.

Our religion, which is so spiritual and sublime, is unjustly accused of countenancing abuses of which there is not the least vestige to be found in the Cathedrals, or old Monasteries.

If men will condescend to hearken to the ignorant, who do not seek instruction, there is not a statue but has spoken, nor

a Saint

a Saint who has not rifen from the dead,
nor a dead perfon whofe apparition has not
been feen; but the enemies of the Catho-
lick religion falfely impute to the Church
of Rome the apocryphal facts to which
fuperftition daily gives vent. It is ufelefs to
preach to the people on that fubject—
they do not eafily recover from their obftinacy, when they perfuade themfelves of
fomething contrary to the doctrines of the
whole Church.

I lately obliged an Englifhman to allow,
that the Proteftants make it their bufinefs
to charge us conftantly with abfurdities
which we reject, and that their method of
judging us is very unfair.

Italy always had fhining Paftors, who lamented the credulity of weak minds, and
the incredulity of Free-thinkers. It is not
from the credulity of the common people
that a fenfible man would judge of the faith
of a country; but from the tenets which
are taught in their catechifms, or in their
public inftructions.

It would very be extraordinary, if Rome,
the Sovereign and Mother of all the
Churches—

Churches—that Rome, the centre of truth and unity, fhould teach abfurdities. My Lord, fhe is juftly vindicated in the work you fent me. I advife you to publifh it, to ftop the mouths of the enemies of the Holy See; and to inform the whole world, that if there are perhaps more inftances of fuperftition in Italy than elfewhere, it is becaufe the people have a more lively imagination, and confequently are more ready to catch, without reflection, at every thing that is prefented to their minds. Take care of your health, notwithftanding the zeal which confumes you, and deign to believe me to be, with infinite refpect,

.   My Lord, &c.

ROME, 17th May, 1751.

L E T-

LETTER XXXVI.

TO CARDINAL QUIRINI.

MOST EMINENT,

THE work I have been reading by your order, is one of the productions of this age, where there are more paradoxes than truths, more objections than folutions, more raillery than proof, more heat than light, more furface than depth. Superficial readers will praife it highly, but men of fenfe will think of it contemptibly; yet as they make the fmalleft number, it is a book which will gain reputation, and make a noife.

Few people know how to value a work. If they are pleafed with the ftyle, they give their fuffrage in its favour, and admire in extafy, without reflecting that the coulouring is the leaft merit of a picture.

It muft be allowed, my Lord, that we live in a whimfical age. There never was lefs religion, but it was never more the fubject of converfation——there never

was

was more wit, nor was ever wit more abufed. Men would know every thing, yet ftudy nothing; they decide upon every thing, but fift nothing to the bottom.

It is not to recriminate, that I exclaim againft the age. They may abufe Priefts, and welcome—I only reproach them for their abufe of Religion. They may have reafon when they complain of our too great numbers, as well as of our taking the vows at too early an age in a profeffion that is to laft for life ; yet if we would enter into the fpirit of any profeffion, we muft engage in it early.

If many of our Paftors would fairly examine themfelves, they would admit, that by their haughtinefs and diffipation they have given room for murmurings and complaints. Wherefore diffemble what all the world knows ? But it is unjuft to make a whole fraternity anfwerable for every one of its individuals, and to confider the fault of one man as the fault of the whole. The fin of a brother is not like original fin, common to all.

You

You fee, my Lord, that I take ample advantage of the liberty your Eminency hath allowed me, to let my pen run on various fubjects, when I have the ineftimable happinefs of writing to you. You know, that being of the order of St. Benedict, we have not always leifure to keep one object in view. The attachment and refpect due to you, is the only object of which we never lofe fight, and it is with that double fentiment that I am

Your Eminency's, &c.

Rome, 3d July, 1751.

––––––––––––

LETTER XXXVII.

TO THE REV. FATHER SIGISMOND OF FERRARA, GENERAL OF THE CAPUCHINS.

Most Rev. Father,

I AM extremely thankful that your apoftolical progrefs has not hindered you from remembering me. I wifh I could have accompanied you; as I am convinced, that on fuch a journey I fhould have received

both

both inftruction and edification. I fhould have admired with you, how much the family of our holy Founder is increafed, and with what richnefs the virtues are perpetuated in your Order,

There is not a good action which the Capuchin Fathers have not done, and there is not an evil with which they can be reproached. The alms given them are a falary juftly due; for they labour with indefatigable zeal both in town and country, for the fupport of Religion, and propagation of the Faith. Capuchins are to be found in the four quarters of the world; they are protected even by the moft barbarous Princes, and are beloved by all nations.

I executed the commiffion you charged me with, at the proper time. I had promifed, and my promifes are inviolable; as I confider their performance to be a duty both of Religion and Morality.

Your garden, my moft Reverend Father, is always one of my favourite walks. I prefer it to the moft magnificent parks: it feems to breathe an air uninfected by the depravity of the times.

I have

I have the honour to be, my moſt Rev.
Father, with all poſſible veneration, &c.

CONVENT of the HOLY APOSTLES,
7th Auguſt, 1751.

LETTER XXXVIII.

TO MADAM B***, A VENETIAN.

MADAM,

YOU do me too much honour when
you aſk my opinion of your admirable tranſlation of Locke.   Is it poſſible,
that in a town plunged as deep in pleaſures as it is in water, a perſon of your
rank ſhould apply herſelf to the depths of
Metaphyſicks? It is an eminent proof, that
our ſoul diſengages itſelf from the ſenſes,
when it would contemplate intellectual objects ; and, conſequently, muſt be incorporeal.

I have read over and over again, with
the ſtricteſt attention, the ineſtimable manuſcript where you have ſo nobly diſplay-
ed

ed the beauties of our language, and with fo much elegance changed the parched field of Philofophy into an agreeable parterre. The Englifh Philofopher would be vain, if he could fee himfelf in his elegant Italian drefs.

I wifh, if it had been poffible, that your Ladyfhip had fuppreffed that part of the work, where Locke hints that matter may have a power of thinking. It is not like the reflection of a Philofopher who has thought deeply. The faculty of thinking cannot be exercifed but by a Being neceffarily endowed with fpiritual and intellectual powers. Matter can never have the privilege of thinking, any more than darknefs can have the power of giving light; both the one and the other imply a contradiction; but men rather choofe to *fpeak abfurdly* than not to fay *uncommon things*.

I congratulate my country more than ever, on its being honoured with a continued fucceffion of learned ladies. It would be very proper to make a collection of thofe works which difplay their fingular abilities,

ties. The tranflation of Locke will hold one of the firft places; efpecially as you have found the fecret of frequently employing the poetick ftyle to foothe the wrinkles of philofophy, which contract the brow, and whofe expreffion is neceffarily hard and dry.

I entreat you, Madam, to print this work, if it be only to convince Foreigners, that fcience is ftill honoured among us, and that your fex are not fo trifling as they are pleafed to imagine.

How could you fingle me out in that crowd, where my fmall fhare of merit has placed me? There are a number of Academicians, efpecially at Bologna, whofe judgement would have been more to be depended on than mine. A man does not commence Philofopher by the profeffion of Philofophy, and efpecially that of *Scotus*, whofe captious fubtlety is nothing but a continual wrangling.

There is more fubftance in one page of our Metaphyficians of the laft age, than in all the books of *Ariftotle* and *Scotus*. The fame cenfure, however, cannot be caft on

5   *Plato*;

Plato ; who in thefe days would have been an excellent Philofopher, and probably a true Chriftian.

I find him full of matter and great views. His refearches, without being ob-fcured by the clouds which furrounded the Ancients, extend to the Deity himfelf.

I could have wifhed, Madam, you had fpared that play of words which difgraces the laft leaves of your tranflation. Trivial decorations are improper in a work of it-felf majeftick. Had Cicero written like Se-neca, he never would have been fo highly efteemed. Pardon my freedom, but you love truth ; and that quality is greater in my eyes, than all the others by which you are adorned.

You will work a great miracle, if you excite a relifh for philofoply at Venice. It is a country where there is a great fhare of genius even among the mechanics ; but pleafure is there, a fifth element, which is a bar to emulation. If we except the order of Senators, who are fo much employed that they may be called the flaves of the nation, the people facrifice to it their

time

time and their reft.   They are always in
gaiety even while they are at work.   But
I perceive that I am infenfibly fpeaking
of government, and that my letter will very foon become guilty of *leze-ferenité*, or
high-treafon againft the ftate.   I know,
that the Moft Serene Republick is very
fcrupulous about what relates to their
ufages and cuftoms, as well as to their
laws.

I will confine myfelf therefore, Madam,
to telling you what will admit of no contradiction, and be entirely conformable to the
fentiments of the whole Senate ; which is,
that they cannot fufficiently affure you of
the refpect due to your genius, your birth,
or your virtue, and with which I have the
honour to be, &c.

Rome, 10th Jan. 1753.

LETTER XXXIX.

TO R. P. LOUIS, OF CREMONA, DIRECTOR
OF THE PIOUS SCHOOLS.

MY REVEREND FATHER,

TO model your preaching after Bour-
daloue is to run the race of immortality.   We want an Orator of your abilities and courage to reform the ftyle of our
pulpits.   In our Sermons, we are rather
Poets than Orators ; and unfortunately
have very frequently more of the *Panto-
mime* than the Pathetic ; while the Word
of God requires the nobleft eloquence, and
the greateft circumfpection.

I am charmed with the manner in which
you have tranflated fome volumes of Bour-
daloue. I do not doubt but our Moft Holy Father will applaud your work with
tranfport; for I know how much he wifhes
for a reformation in our Sermons. He
does not require that Italian eloquence
fhould become French —every language
has its peculiar turns and expreffions ; but
he wifhes that our preachers would fpeak
the

the language of Christians, which ought
to be evangelical, and which should never
be disfigured by burlesque.

The mouth of the Preacher is truely the
mouth of God. Alas! then, what is to be
thought of him who can utter buffoon-
ries and trifles from the pulpit?

Whoever does not find in the Holy
Scriptures, and the Works of the Fathers,
wherewithal to affect his hearers, is not
worthy of mounting the pulpit. There
cannot be finer images of the greatness and
mercy of God, than in the Psalms and Spiritual Songs—there cannot be more affecting histories than those of Joseph, of
Moses, and of the Maccabees—there cannot be more striking examples of the Divine Justice, than the punishment of Na-
dab and Abihu, or of Belshazzar, who saw
a dreadful hand writing in tremendous
characters his condemnation on the wall.

In all the books of the world you cannot find such strains of eloquence as the
reflections of Job; all attempts to para-
phrase only enervate them. Delightful
discourses may be composed by selecting

some

fome of the moſt beautiful paſſages in
Scripture, and adapting them to the ſubject. St. Paul, the moſt pathetic and ſublime of all Preachers, employed only the
language of the Scriptures in his Epiſtles,
and they are admirable.

We ſhould burn the greateſt part of our
Sermons, to prevent the taſte of our young
Preachers from being corrupted. There
they ſearch for apocryphal facts, Pagan
citations, and thence form to themſelves a
ſtyle truely ridiculous. Sentiments of compunction or terrour, which are produced by
the exclamations, grimace, and geſtures of
the Preacher, make but momentary im-
preſſions. They are ſtrokes of thunder,
which aſtoniſh, and may cauſe the audi-
ence to make the ſign of the Croſs *, but
do not prevent their laughing the inſtant
after.

If your method, Moſt Rev. Father, can
be introduced among us, you will be the
reſtorer of Chriſtian eloquence, and all
who feel it will bleſs you.

I had

* The people in Italy make the ſign of the Croſs
when they hear thunder.

I had for a ghoftly Father a Monk, who was filled with the Spirit of God, and who was grieved every time he heard fome Preachers : but when he himfelf preached, it was his heart which fpoke, and confequently his hearers were deeply affected.

I fhall fee you with great pleafure, when you honour me with a vifit ; I fhall have nothing to do then but to liften.

I endeavour in the midft of my daily occupations to have always fome moments for myfelf and for my friends. The foul has need of fome refpite, that it may the better purfue its labours. The fciences are mountains, which we cannot climb without taking breath.

Take care of yourfelf : but lefs upon your own account than our's, who wifh to read, hear, and admire you. It is with that defire fo conformable to Religion and the wifhes of my country, that I have the honour to be, in the fullnefs of my heart,

Your moft humble, &c.

Convent of the Holy Apostles,
      3d March, 1755.

K 3   P. S.

P. S. As to a reform in the Breviary, which you mentioned to me, I wish our Holy Father would think seriously of it. However, I am not of your opinion as to the distribution of the Psalms. I should think it proper, if I was consulted, to leave the *Beati immaculati in viâ* to be repeated daily. It is a continual protestation of an inviolable attachment to the Law of God, and which is better in the mouths of the Ministers of God, than some obscure enigmatical Psalms, which are often unintelligible to the generality of Priests.

I would likewise leave the Prayer-Book as it is. You will tell me, that any set form of words becomes too much a thing of course to preserve its effect; but are we not exposed to the same inconvenience with regard even to the prayers of the Mass, when it is celebrated every day?

The notes you sent me on the *Imitation of Jesus Christ* are admirable.

LETTER XL.

TO COUNT ***.

I OWE you a Library, my dear friend, but you shall pay for it. I promised to give you a lift of the books which I think neceffary for you, and now I muft acquit my-felf of my promife. This lift fhall be fhort, becaufe it is not the multitude of books which makes us learned. It is of no con-fequence to read much; but it is of effential importance to read well.

The book which I would place at the head of your library is the *Gospel*, as the moft neceffary and the moft facred. It is right that the book which contains the principles and bafis of Religion fhould be the foundation of your ftudies.

There you will learn to know what you owe to God, and to the wifdom and good-nefs of the Mediator in whom we hope, and who hath reconciled Heaven and Earth by the fhedding of his blood..

That book has been in your hands almoft from your infancy; but as you attended but little to it then, it will now excite new fentiments in your foul. The Gofpel, when meditated upon with due refpect, fhows itfelf to be the language of God. You will not find in it that oratorical emphafis which characterifes Rhetoricians; thofe fyllogiftical arguments which mark the Philofophers—it is quite fimple, all is within the reach of every capacity, and all is divine.

I exprefsly recommend to you to read St. Paul's Epiftles. Befides infpiring you with an averfion againft falfe teachers and falfe devotees, who under an appearance of fanctity deftroy the fpirit of it, they will infpire you with univerfal charity, which comprehends all Religion; and which, better than all the Preceptors in the world, makes us good relations, good friends, and good citizens. At the fchool of the Apoftle we learn all the œconomy of Religion; *its length, its depth, its fublimity;* in a word, *the moft excellent fcience of Jefus Chrift,* who would be univerfally adored, if he

was

was more generally known, and by whom the intellectual and material worlds were made.

Your conſtant manuel ought to be the Pſalter, as dictated by the Holy Spirit; a work which warms the ſoul while it enlivens the mind, and which for the true ſublime, ſurpaſſes all the Orators or Poets that ever wrote.

I would not recommend to you to take too great a portion of theſe writings at a time. The Holy Scriptures ſhould not be peruſed but with reflection and reſerve; for beſides that every text affords matter for ample meditation, the Word of God deſerves another kind of reſpect than the words of men.

Take care to procure the *Confeſſions of St. Auguſtine*, a book written with his tears; but it is a work better calculated for the heart than the head; and you ſhould attend to it in that light. To this you ſhould join the collection of ſelect pieces from the Fathers of the Church, ſo as to know of yourſelf, that Chriſtian eloquence alone can truely elevate the ſoul, and that

it.

it is a thoufand times more fublime than all profane Oratory, becaufe it has for its object God himfelf, the fountain of all greatnefs.

The Imitation of Jefus Chrift is a book much too pious and inftructive to be left out of your Catalogue. Notwithftanding what all the writers of Diflertations have faid upon this head, it is an Italian production; for Gerfon, Abbé of Verceil, is the Author. And in it the foul will find whatever can edify or comfort her. Make frequent ufe of it, as the work in the world the moft fertile in confolations for every fituation in life.

Study carefully the *Introduction to the Chriftian Doctrine*, a work of P. Gerdil, a Barnabite, as it is a book which you cannot read too often; and intermix the Hiftory of the Church with that of Empires and Nations, fo as not to confufe your mind and ideas. The head fhould be always clear, when we are to judge with wifdom and precifion. When you become better acquainted with the French language, I advife you to

read

read Boffuet's Univerfal Hiftory ; and the Thoughts of Pafchal on Religious Truths.

The Annals of Italy by the immortal Muratori, the Hiftory of Naples by Giannone, the Campaigns of Don Carlos by Buonamici, the periodical publications of the Abbé Lami, (which laft I recommend not to teach you to decide, but to think rightly) are fo many works which you ought to perufe.

I do not mention books of natural hiftory and antiquities, though they are fubjects of which no one fhould be ignorant.

You muft remember, my dear friend, that Cicero, Virgil, and Horace trod the ground which we inhabit ; that they breathed the fame **air** which we breathe ; and that as they are our countrymen, we fhould read their writings from time to time, efpecially as they are filled with elegant inftruction. You have made good proficiency in claffical learning, and it will be eafy **for** you occafionally to enjoy their agreeable converfation.

I do not debar you from reading our modern Poets, provided you perufe them with precaution, and do not go to throw your-

K 6   felf

felf headlong into all their labyrinths, their grottoes, and their groves : thefe are not proper places for a Chriftian foul. I do not like that you fhould remain too long with the fabulous Goddeffes ; thefe are fictions which lead too often to realities.

I fhould be much better pleafed to fee Pliny's Letters, the Meditations of Marcus Aurelius or of Seneca in your hands ; there you will find fentiments of humanity that cannot be too much commended.

Behold, my dear friend, the whole of the Library I would confine you to; becaufe I think we fhould have books only for ufe, and not for oftentation. You may add Cardinal Bentivoglio's Letters.

I neither give you legends, nor myfticks. You will find the principal Saints in the Hiftory of the church ; and the account which is given of them in the apocryphal books, would perhaps only ferve to make you doubt of the wonders they really wrought, and leffen the refpect which is due to them. Great men fhould not be feen but in the great, and truth needs no fupport to make it refpected.

If

If I have not mentioned books of philofophy to you, it is becaufe I would not
fend you back to fchool to adopt fyftems,
and learn to difpute. I am afraid you
might pick up fome whimfical notion or
other; and to fpeak impartially, I would
not have you efpoufe any one opinion of
the Schools.

Philofophy has produced more fophiftry
than found reafoning; and to be a true
philofopher it is fufficient that you have a
perfect knowledge of the Heavens and the
Earth, a clear and precife idea of our duties, our origin, and our deftiny. In the
midft of your exercifes and your ftudies
reflect upon thefe great objects; and when
you have determined upon your profeffion
in life, you will then be informed how to
inftruct youfelf in what relates to it.

Good night!—My pen cannot go farther; my head, fatigued by continual application through the whole day, obliges
me to ftop here. It is only my heart that
I find always in full vigour, when it is
employed in affuring you how much

I am, &c.

ROME, 31ft Dec, 1751.

L E T-

LETTER XLI.

TO CARDINAL PASSIONEI.

MOST EMINENT,

IF we could make reftitution of our knowledge, as we can of goods we had ftolen, your Eminency would fee me laying at your feet all the fcience I am poffeffed of, as your own property; and then there would be no room to praife me for my pretended knowledge. Almoft every Saturday I go to your Eminency's magnificent Library, and fill myfelf as much as I can with whatever excellent things fall in my way. I come there quite indigent, but return exceffively rich – fo that my reputation and merit are founded upon thefe fecret robberies; and it is to your books, my Lord, not to my own genius, that I am indebted.

I fhare in the pleafures they tafte who hear your Eminency in that delightful hermitage, where Science prefides, where Vir-

tue

tue fhines, and Friendfhip holds converfe.
It is decreed that Brother Ganganelli muft
confine his wifhes to fuch a gratification ;
for his employment will never allow him
to go and repofe himfelf under the fhade
of your myrtle and orange trees.—That
would be too fenfual for a monk of St.
Francis, who ought to know nothing but
mortification and poverty.

What comforts me, my Lord, is, that
happily I tafte the pureft pleafure in fulfilling the tafk which is prefcribed me ;
and the refpects which I fhould otherwife
prefent to you at Frefcati, could neither
be more profound nor extenfive, than
thofe with which I have the honour to be
here, &c.

ROME, 8th May, 1753.

LETTER XLII.

TO M. AYMALDI.

THE laſt memorial which you ſent me, reſembles thoſe uncultivated countries where there are by chance ſome agreeable ſpots. I unravelled it with Monkiſh patience, and with the greateſt deſire to oblige you. There would be too great pleaſure in ſtudying, if we were to meet with nothing but flowers. Every man who is employed in his cloſet ſhould look upon himſelf as a traveller, who ſometimes travels through flowery paths, and ſometimes meets with rugged roads.

That light production of P. Nocetti the Jeſuit, upon the *Iris*, abounds with delicacy. You find there that brilliant and poetick imagination which embelliſhes the thoughts and the ſtyle. The Jeſuits have always cultivated the Belles-Lettres with ſuccefs. Theſe kinds of writing are like vivifying waters to me; they recall my vital ſpirits when I find myſelf exhauſted

with

with painful ftudies—I fmell to them, and
recover my ftrength.   You know that Science is the grave of the Belles-Lettres, if
we do not fpare them a few hours, now-
and-then, to prevent our forgetting them.
My Profeffor of Theology faid to me, once,
" I am fo abforbed in abftrufe ftudies, that
" my mind lofes the relifh for more polite
" performances."—Tafte itfelf becomes
blunted, if we give it nothing to relifh.

I fhall fee the R. P. General of the Do-
minicans (P. Bremond) on the fubject of
your affair, and I believe I fhall fucceed.
Befides his being very obliging in his own
nature, he bears great good-will to me ;
and I fhall likewife remind him, that St.
Francis and St. Dominick being good
friends, and alfo St. Bonaventure and St.
Thomas Aquinas, it is proper that the
fame happy harmony fhould fubfift among
their Difciples.

Adieu ! Take care of your health ; for
we may wager any thing, that during the
Pontificate of a learned man your merit
muft lead to great things.   I do not wifh

it

it so much on your account, or my own, as for the honour of the Holy See.

I have that of being, &c.

ROME, 12th May, 1753.

LETTER XLIII.

TO DOM GAILLARD, PRIOR OF THE CHARTREUX AT ROME.

MY REV. FATHER,

SINCE you have opened your heart to me about what passes in your Community, I will open mine to you with the same candour; and must tell you, that in an Order so rigid as your's, it were much to be wished the Superiors were more communicative; that they should not let a week pass without visiting their Monks; that they ought to insinuate themselves amicably into their hearts, and by salutary advice and tender encouragement assist them to support the yoke of solitude.

The

The kingdom of Christ is not the empire of despotism. It is both contrary to Religion and Humanity to render men slaves. If a person has made a vow to obey his Superiors, he has not engaged to respect their caprices.

It is generally imagined, that the office of Superior is a place of authority, which consists in commanding, and seeing the Monks trembling and submissive. But the Chief of a community is a person who should be *all things to all men*; he ought to study their different characters, sound their geniuses, and know what is hurtful to one, what is useful to another, and what every one in particular is capable of.

There are some Monks who have no desire for conversation, because they are naturally of a silent temper; there are others whom an obstinate silence would render miserable, because they are of a sociable disposition; and in such a situation a Superior should have different ways of conducting himself, excusing one rather than the other, if they should make some flight

flight infractions of the rules. Every Religious Order ought to be of the temper of our Saviour, who was always gentle and of humble heart; who treated his Disciples as brethren and friends, calling himself their servant, and actually performing the functions of a servant.

Rules would be like a step-mother, if they punished unmercifully those who by too great vivacity, or too great slowness, should become guilty of some omissions. There are Monks whom a Superior should visit more frequently, because they are more frequently tempted, and find it more difficult to endure retirement: so that without a spirit of discernment and penetration, a Superior would be only an image, whose government must be contemptible. There is only one way of directing, and yet there are as many different directions necessary, as there are individuals in the Community. One falls off from his duty, if reprimanded; while another shall double his diligence, if he finds the flightest lapse animadverted upon.

The

The Order of the Chartreux deferves all possible respect, as having had no occasion either for change of discipline, or for reformation, during the seven centuries that it hath subsisted; but I confess to you, that the Priors have always appeared to me to have affected too sullen and severe a deportment, and by going singly to the general Chapters, made themselves both judges and parties.

As they frequently receive visits, and have the liberty of writing and going abroad themselves, they should not be too strict against a poor Monk for letting a few words escape his lips.

They become inquisitors in their office, when they would punish every thing, and overlook nothing. There are petty wranglings in Communities as well as in families, which subsist only because their Superiors do not know how to despise them.

Visit your Brotherhood in friendship— do not speak to them of the past, and you will see them ashamed of having caballed. Nothing disarms rage so much as gentleness—in embracing them with cordiality,

you

you will fhow them that you can conquer yourfelf, and they will be edified. There is nothing more dangerous for people in office, than never to allow that they have been miftaken.

Accuftom yourfelf to reform the faults of your Monks in your own Houfe, without informing the General of them. Such a conduct irritates thofe that are accufed, and fhows a want of the proper talent for governing.

This is my way of thinking. If I am deceived, you will do me a pleafure by proving it—if your reafons are good, I will fubmit ; for I am neither prejudiced in my own favour, nor obftinate in my opinions. It is my heart only that fpeaks throughout this letter ; and it is that alfo which affures you of the fincerity of thofe fentiments with which

I am, &c.

Rome, 21ft of June, 1754.

LETTER XLIV.

TO THE SAME.

THE *fiesto*, or afternoon's nap of Italy, my moft dear and reverend Father, would not have alarmed you fo much, if you had recollected, that when we are at Rome, we fhould do **as** the Romans do — *Cum Romano Romanus eris.*

Is it either fin **or** fhame, **then, for a** poor Monk, in a country where one is op-preffed with exceffive heat, to indulge in half an hour's repofe, that he may after-wards purfue his exercifes with the more activity? Confider, that filence **is** beft kept when one is afleep. You, who reckon among the capital fins, the pronouncing a fingle word **when** your Rules forbid the ufe of fpeech, take the example of Chrift when he found his Apoftles afleep: *Alas!* fays he to them, with the greateft mildnefs, *could you not watch with me one hour?*

5   But

But how can you confiftently expect from your Monks, the obedience which you refufe to the Sovereign Pontiff? You cannot but know, that all the Monaftick laws owed their force only to the approbation of the Popes; and if he, who reigns at prefent with fo much wifdom, were pleafed to give your Monks a difpenfation from certain cuftoms, it is abfolutely in his power. There is no contending with the Legiflator the right of modifying the laws.

The foftening fome aufterities which depend upon time, place, and circumftance, does not affect the effence of the vows. *The latter kill, but the fpirit brings to life.* But there are fome reftlefs Superiors who are afraid left they fhould omit a fyllable of the Conftitutions. For God's fake, be calm, both for the good of your Monks and your own health. While you confult me, I muft reply in this manner: It is not fufficient to alledge the dictates of confcience, unlefs it be enlightened. I embrace you with all my heart, being, &c.

ROME, 21ft Sept: 1754.

L E T-

LETTER XIV.

TO A MONK SETTING OUT FOR AMERICA.

THE feas will very foon feparate us; but fuch is the lot of this life, that fome are fcattered to the extremities of the world, while others remain always in the fame place. One thing is certain, that my heart follows your's :—and that wherever your's fhall be, there will mine be found alfo.

If you have not laid in an ample ftock of piety, I fhall be exceedingly in fear for you, on a paffage where all the words you hear will not be thofe of edification; and in a country where all the examples pre- fented to you, will not be found the moft correct models of virtue.   America is the earthly Paradife where they frequently eat the forbidden fruit. The ferpent is conti- nually preaching upon the love of riches and pleafures, and the warmth of the cli- mate fets the paffions in commotion.

VOL. I.   L   We

We are unfortunate enough in this world not to be able to reftrain our paffions, when we perceive no other Superior but God, unlefs a lively Faith be the principle of our actions. And fuch is the cafe of the **Religious who live in America.** Not having any Superior, who has a right to prefcribe rules, or any authority to exact their obfervance, they are loft, if the Gofpel does not reign in their hearts.

. I perfuade myfelf, that you will frequently beg of God to give you ftrength to fupport you againft all kinds of dangers. **Much good effect may be** produced, even among the **Negroes,** notwithftanding their being generally addicted to the groffeft **vices,** provided a **Paftor** can contrive to gain their confidence, and be able to imprefs their minds with a certain awe.

Think that the God of the univerfe will be as near you in America, as in Europe; that his eye feeth every where, his juftice judgeth all; and that it is for him alone you ought to act. Lead a diligent and regular life; for, unfortunately, fhould you
once

once be poſſeſſed by a ſpirit of indolence, you will ſoon be beſet by the Vices, without being able to defend yourſelf.

Never ſuffer one word to paſs your lips which can be interpreted againſt Religion or Morals. Even thoſe who ſeemingly applaud, will, in fact, deſpiſe you, as an unworthy ſervant, who makes a mock of the Maſter whoſe bread he eats, and whoſe livery he wears.

God preſerve you from heaping up riches! A Prieſt who loves money, but eſpecially a Monk who has taken the vow of poverty, is worſe than the wicked rich man, and deſerves to be ſtill more rigorouſly treated.

Be ſociable, and gain your pariſhioners' affections by much affability :—let them ſee that you are actuated by true piety, not by caprice.

Do not meddle in ſecular affairs, except to accommodate law-ſuits, and reſtore peace. I will pray for you to Him who commands the waves, who calms the tempeſts, and who doth not abandon his people where-ever found. What comforts me

is,

is, that fouls know no diftance; for by the ties of Religion and the heart, we are always neighbours to one another.

Adieu, and adieu! I tenderly embrace you.

LETTER XLVI.

TO THE PRELATE CERATI.

YOU are too happy, my dear Prelate, in dividing your time between Pifa and Florence :—in the one, your mind is at its eafe; and in the other, your knowledge finds its proper fuftenance.

When I refleét that Tufcany is truely the reftorer of Arts and Sciences, I greatly revere it, and feel my heart palpitate every time I hear it mentioned. The advantage of the happieft fituation and happieft climate rendered it worthy of this glory; we breathe a fweetnefs of air there, which feems to give the foul a new being; and it is perceivable at every ftep, why the Fine

Arts

Arts chofe that fituation for their refidence.

I knew an old man of the moft cultivated
reafon, and the moft voluptuous mind,
who arranged his time fo well, that he paffed the fpring every year at Pifa, the fummer at Sienna, the autumn at Leghorn,
and the winter at Florence. He went al-
ternately to thefe four towns, to ftudy the
humour of the inhabitants, to give vent to
his own, and to tafte the fweets of the moft
agreeable fociety. Our Converfations begin to degenerate—they have loft that
fpirit with which our fathers fupported
them; and it is to the too agreeable French
frivolity, which captivates all minds, that
we are indebted to the change.

Every Age bears fome characteriftick
mark—luxury, which corrupts our morals, corrupts likewife our difcourfe and our
writings; there is fcarce any foul in our
converfation, in our writings, or our paintings. We poffefs nothing now but a certain elegance, as fuperficial as the genius
which produces it; and unfortunately
even Religion partakes of this evil. We

think

think we can take whatever is difpleafing from Chriftianity, as we can retrench the ornaments of drefs.

You are fenfible of thefe evils :—you lament, and you have reafon.

I have the honour to be, &c.

Rome, 2d Sept. 1754.

LETTER XLVII.

TO THE ABBE CAMILLAC, AUDITOR OF ROTA.

I CALLED upon you, my Lord, that I might have the honour of delivering with my own hand a volume of Monf. Buffon—an excellent book; an excellent writer, if he was not too fyftematical: there is an energy in his ftyle and his thoughts which tranfports and aftonifhes the Reader. To afk my opinion of the liberties of the Gallican Church, is to put it out of my power to fpeak. Befides, what fignifies that queftion, if the French, like the Romans, are Catholicks, notwithftanding the fentiments which divide them upon this article? The Popes and the Kings in times

paft

paft were reciprocally wrong, and Benedict XIV. is happily the moft proper Pontiff to make their errours be for ever forgotten.

What you have deigned to recommend to me fhall be done as foon as poffible, with a zeal equal to the refpect with which

I am, &c.

ROME, 6th June, 1754.

LETTER XLVIII.

TO THE MARQUIS SCIPIO MAFFEI.

THE young Monk whom you recommended to me is quite vain of fuch an honour, and I am no lefs fo of your excellent letter: I fhall preferve it as a talifman to communicate to me fome fparks of your learning and genius. I would fay a thoufand things, but am afraid of you as of a fpirit, and find myfelf interdicted. I recollect the immenfity of your knowledge, and the merit of your productions; and that rememberance renders me fo little in my own eyes, that I cannot appear before you.

L 4

Italy

Italy will long be vain of having given you birth; and if Verona knew its glory, it would erect ftatues to you; but what renders you fuperior to fuch vain honours, is, that you are the humbleft of men, and know lefs than any man your own worth.

I would not pardon Time, who, without refpect to merit, brings on old age, if I was not perfuaded with you, that a heavenly life awaits us. We know that Heaven is the centre and habitation of all light, and that the knowledge which is acquired there in a moment, exceeds beyond the reach of comparifon the feeble glimmerings which we enjoy here below.

I fhall pay all poffible attention to your recommendation. He fhall become my fon, as he has been your's, by the intereft I fhall take in his improvement, both in the fciences and in piety. He will find in our Order the fame affiftance which I found there, to inftruct and form me; and I can fay, upon this occafion, without flattering my brethren, that he could not be better fituated for thofe purpofes. They have a

tafte

tafte for good authors; they encourage emulation; they give conftant application; and they efteem, in a moft particular manner, the incomparable Scipio Maffei. He lives in our hearts as he does in his own writings; and this I can certainly affure him of, being more than any one, &c.

LETTER XLIX.

TO MONS. CARACCIOLI, NUNCIO AT VENICE, AND LATE NUNCIO IN SPAIN.

My Lord,

I HAVE the honour of fending you the refolution of the Holy Office, which will certainly be agreeable to your manner of thinking. I have expreffed in it all the zeal that I am capable of, to prove to you the infinite efteem I have of your worth. I wifh the Church always had Prelates as exemplary as your Lordfhip! It is what the Venetians often fay, and what tranfports me with joy, when I have a happy opportunity of affuring you of all the refpect with which I am, &c.

R. me, 2 ft Oct. 1754.

L 5

LET-

LETTER L.

TO COUNT ***.

IF you be feifed with fcruples, my dear friend, you are ruined; you will either relapfe into diffipation, or ferve God like a flave. Remember that the Jewifh law was a law of fear, but the new law is a law of love. The veffel of clay to which our fouls are attached, does not allow of angelical perfection.

Religion is degraded, when we apply our attention to trifles. While men pray, there will be inattentions; as long as men act, there will be errours in conduct, becaufe every man is fubject to vanity and error—*Omnis homo mendax.*

None but falfe devotees are fcandalized at every thing, and fee the Devil every where. Fulfil the law without labouring in fpirit, and without ftraining the imagination, and you will render yourfelf agreeable to God. Nothing checks the foul in the road to piety, fo much as fcruples ill

underftood

underftood. As too much retirement encourages gloomy notions, and fociety dif-
pels them, frequent rational company, and
live but little alone—Be not difcouraged
when you feel yourfelf tempted. Temp-
tation is a trial which teaches us to diftruft
ourfelves, and adds to our merits when it
is conquered.

Come and fee me, and we will endeavour together to find out the fource of
thofe doubts which torment you. I have
nothing more at heart than to be affured
you are a good Chriftian; but I fhall be
unhappy if you give way to fcruples; for
then every thing will alarm you, and you
will become infupportable to yourfelf.

I have always forgot to fpeak to you
about our worthy relation. See what fad
tricks my abfence of mind fometimes plays
me; but the heart has no fhare in the
omiffion. The Marchionefs, more ftartled
than penetrated with my remonftrances,
does not know how to act.—When a devotee once hefitates about a reconciliation,
you muft expect only doubtful proofs of
it: but as we take what we can get of a bad

debt, fo fhould you take in good part the flighteft marks of politenefs that your dear Coufin may henceforward think proper to fhow you.

Perfevere, my dear friend, perfevere. I am edified by your courage, and happy that you are pleafed with the guide I have given you. Is he not a worthy man, and one that will certainly lead you to Heaven? He has a wonderful fkill in difcovering people's difpofitions, and is the man in the world the moft proper for gaining their confidence.

I approve of what you lay afide for charitable purpofes; but I do not love beftowing drop by drop, or tying one's-felf down to regular alms-giving, fo as to have nothing left for an object in extreme want. It is better to refcue one or two families from diftrefs, than to fcatter a few pieces at random, without completing any purpofe. Befides, it would be proper to have always a fum in referve for extraordinary cafes; for by this œconomy you will have a remedy at hand for unforefeen contingencies.

Do

Do not give into that wrong notion of charity, which, without confidering either birth or extraction, clothes and feeds all its objects like the meaneft of the people.

Charity humbles nobody, and fhould be proportioned to circumftances and conditions. To give haughtily, is worfe than to with-hold. Diftribute your alms in fuch a manner as to appear more humble yourfelf than they who receive. Religion is too noble to approve of thofe little fouls who oblige with infolence, and make the importance of their fervices be felt.

Be not content with giving, but, according to the precepts of the Scripture, lend likewife to him that is in need. I do not know a more contemptible object than money, if it be not employed to affift our neighbour. Can the infipid pleafure of heaping up a few crowns, be compared with the fatisfaction of conferring happinefs, and the felicity of attaining Heaven?

When you are become an œconomift without avarice, and generous without prodigality, I fhall look upon you as *a rich man who can be faved*. Prevent wants, without

out waiting till you be afked : true charity can divine.

Adieu !—It appears fuperfluous to repeat, at the end of this letter, that I am your beft friend and humble fervant. Certainly you do not doubt it, or you affront me moft fenfibly.

ROME, 19th of April, 1752.

LETTER LI.

TO THE SAME

YOU afk me, why, at fome times, we fink into melancholy without knowing the caufe, and become a burthen to ourfelves ? To which I anfwer,

Firft, It is becaufe we are dependent upon a body which is not always in perfect equilibrium.

Secondly, Becaufe God Almighty would make us fenfible that this life is not the fcene of our happinefs, and that we fhall always be ill at eafe till we leave it;

and

and it was for that reason the Apostle long-
ed after the things that are eternal.

There are fogs in the moral as well as
in the natural world; and the foul, like
the ſky, hath its clouds.

The beſt way to diſpel ſuch glooms, is
to ſeek employment. When ſeriouſly occupied, we have not leiſure to become either
melancholy or languid. Study is the element of the mind. *If you love ſtudy*, ſaid
Seneca, *you will neither be a burthen to yourſelf nor to others.* It is inconceivable how
many wretched quarters of hours there are
in life, from which employment would defend us. You cannot be happy in this
world, but by knowing how to blunt the
edge of your ſorrows. He who has no
vexation at preſent, either has had or will
have ſome; becauſe pain and ſorrow are
an inheritance from our firſt father, and
we cannot entirely preſerve ourſelves from
them.

I am with all my heart, &c.

Rome, 27th April, 1752.

L E T-

LETTER LII.

TO MONSIGNOR FIRNIANI, BISHOP OF PERUSA.

MY LORD,

THE Candidate you recommend to me feems to prefer the Order of the Auguftines to that of the Francifcans; and far from being diffatisfied at it, I have juft now been to conduct him to a Monk, who is one of my friends; he will take all poffible care of him, and after a proper tryal, will give him the habit of St. Auguftine.

Provided we bring with us the true fpirit of piety, it is no matter in what Convent we are placed. All the different Orders make but one and the fame family in my eyes: and happily I have no partiality for my own Community to the prejudice of another. Befides, the Auguftines have always connected knowledge with virtue; and no man, whofe heart is well difpofed, can fail to receive excellent inftructions among them.

The

The P. Capuchin, who fpoke to your Lordſhip fo favourably of me, has feen but little of me; he judges of me as of a diſtant landſcape, which is imagined to be fomething fine on a nearer view, but is found to be nothing extraordinary. I will oblige him to recant when he returns to Rome, becauſe he ſhall then fee me as I really am. It is the beſt way that I know of correcting the miſtaken notions which men may have formed of my abilities. I recommend myſelf to your prayers, which I believe to be moſt effectual before God, and I have the honour to be, &c.

Rome, 26th Aug. 1753.

LETTER LIII.

TO THE PRELATE CERATI.

MY LORD,

I HAVE juſt now been to fee your good old friend, M. Bottari, and found him, as uſual, immerſed in the deepeſt and moſt intereſting ſtudies. He paſſed from

them

them to a picturefque converfation, which delighted me exceffively; for he does not fpeak, he paints. He is fententious and figurative; and never fails perfectly to characterife the books and perfons he defcribes.

We had a good deal of difcourfe about the Roman Antiquities, and the variety of our Libraries, which, though not all of equal excellence, form an admirable collection. Two well informed Englifhmen fhared in our converfation, and fpoke fo as to demand attention. They are a people that travel to advantage, profiting by whatever they fee. They are faid to take the fubftance of things, while the French are content with the furface. But I leave you to decide, whether for commerce with mankind, it is better to be fuperficial and agreeable, or profound and gloomy.

Cardinal Bentivoglio faid, *that we fhould fee an Englifhman when we want to think, and a Frenchman when we want to converfe.*

I open my cell to both one and the other with the greateft pleafure, always confeffing to you, that the French vivacity has
fome-

fomething very attracting for me. We love to meet our own likenefs; and you know that I am neither flow nor filent.

You doubtlefs have received the book which P. Maffoleni of the Order of the Oratory fent you. You will find it both interefting and well executed. Methinks I fee you plunged into this work, without being able to tear yourfelf from it. The retired man has real pleafures, which fur-pafs all the joys of the world. But hufh! that is a fecret of the ftudious, which fhould not be divulged.

I have the honour to be, &c.

ROME, 13th Nov. 1753.

LETTER LIV.

TO A FRANCISCAN FRIAR.

I FEEL fomething within me which makes me take pen in hand, and whif-pers in my ear to write to you, that it is a great while fince I have had that exquifite pleafure;

4

pleafure; and it is my friendfhip for you which procures it me at prefent.

It muft be confeffed, as St. Auguftine fays, *that friendfhip has fomething in it very charming, and that the perfon who is unac-quainted with its delights fhould be excluded from fociety.* The Saviour of the world hath canonifed it, by his particular attach-ment to St John; and we fee that the greateft Saints have cultivated it with the moft religious attention.

Continue to be always my good friend. Although the world fays that Monks love nobody, I have found the moft fincere and friendly hearts in the Cloifter:—yet the world will believe nothing of this, becaufe it will have us to be wrong in every thing; but what fignifies that to us, while we tafte the fweets of fuch a fympathy, and I continue no lefs than ever,

Your friend and fervant.

Rome, 29th Dec. 1754.

LET-

LETTER LV.

TO LADY PIGLIANI.

THE domeſtic education of your two daughters is no indifferent matter: —the condition of a mother impoſes on you the moſt important duties. The world will continually interpoſe between you and your children, if you do not take care to keep it at a diſtance—not with auſterity, which excites only murmuring, but with that prudence which gains confidence.

Your daughters will only prove hypocrites, if you perplex and incumber them with inſtructions; inſtead of which they will love Religion, if you know how to make them do ſo by your example, and by your gentleneſs.

Girls of twenty are not to be uſed as if they were but ten; there is a treatment and method of Inſtruction ſuited to different ages, as well as to different conditions of life.

Encourage

Encourage a taſte for good Authors, and for employment as much as you can; but with that freedom which does not tie them down to the minute; and with that ſpirit of diſcernment which knows how to diſtinguiſh what is proper for a ſecular houſe, from what would more fitly become a Cloiſter.

Eſtabliſh your daughters according to their fortunes and rank, without reſtraining their inclinations, unleſs they ſhould tend to diſſipation or folly. Marriage is the natural condition of mankind; but there are exceptions to this rule, when it may be diſpenſed with.

Without being in love with the vanities of the world, do not make yourſelf ridiculous, by oppoſing the cuſtoms of the times. Piety becomes a ſubjeĉt of raillery, when it appears to affeĉt ſingularity; a prudent woman ſhould avoid rendering herſelf remarkable.

When a woman is born to a certain rank of life, ſhe ſhould dreſs ſuitably to her pretenſions; but ſtill within that line which modeſty and decency preſcribe.

See

See that your daughters mix in good company. True devotion is neither ruſtic nor auſtere. Solitude ill employed irritates the paſſions, and it is often better for young people to ſee well choſen company, than to remain alone. You ſhould inſpire them with chearfulneſs, that they may not aſſume a ſanctified air. Their recreations ſhould be walking, and little innocent paſtimes; and when you come to talk of application, do not mention deep ſtudies, nor abſtract ſciences, which often make the ſex vain and talkative.

Above all things, make yourſelf beloved; it is the greateſt pleaſure that a mother can aſpire to, and the greateſt prerogative ſhe can enjoy, in order to affect the good ſhe purpoſes.

Take care that your domeſticks be religious and honeſt; if they do not fear God, they are capable of every thing that is bad. They ſhould not be treated either with haughtineſs or familiarity, but as people who are of the ſame nature, though your inferiors. Juſtice is the mother of Order: every thing is in its proper place, when we act with equity.

Never

Never punish but with regret, and always pardon wth pleafure.

Frequent your Parifh Church, that the fheep may be often found with their Paftor; it is a practice conformable to the holy Canons, as well as of ancient ufage.

Your own wifdom will teach you the reft. I depend much upon your underftanding and good-will, as you may be affured of the refpectful confideration with which I have the honour to be, &c.

Rome, 15th Nov. 1754.

LETTER LVI.

TO COUNT ALGAROTTI.

My dear Count,

MANAGE matters fo, that notwithftanding your Philofophy, I may fee you in Heaven; for I fhould be exceedingly grieved to lofe fight of you for an eternity.

You are one of thofe fingular men, both in head and heart, whofe friendfhip we would wifh to continue beyond the grave, when we have the pleafure of knowing them; and furely nobody has more rea- fons than you to be perfuaded that the foul is incorporeal and immortal. Years pafs away for the Philofopher, as they do for the Fool; but in what they are to termi- nate, muft engage the mind of a thinking man.

Confefs that I know how to accommo- date my fermons, fo as not to ftartle one of the *beaux-efprits*: and if difcourfes were more frequently made with as much brevi- ty and friendfhip, you would fometimes, perhaps, liften to the Preachers.—But it is not enough to hear them; what is faid fhould find its way to the heart.—May it produce good fruit there; and may the amiable Algarotti become as good a Chri- ftian as he is a Philofopher, and then I fhall be doubly his friend and fervant!

ROME, 11th Dec. 1754.

LETTER LVII.

TO MONSIGNOR ROTA, DECIPHERER,

I BELIEVE, my Lord, that in order to render it poffible for us to meet, it is neceffary to make an appointment.—I beg of you to fix the hour, and moft certainly I will not fail to attend you.

There is no time I regret the lofs of fo much, as that which is fpent in anti-chambers. Time is the moft precious gift which God hath given us, and man diffipates it with a profufion equally extravagant and unaccountable.

Alas! time is a property expofed to be pillaged, and every one robs us of a part. In fpite of all my care to preferve it, I fee it flip through my hands, and I can fcarcely fay that it flies, before it is already gone.

I wait your orders to attend you, and to tell you, if there are any moments in which you are to be feen, that there are none in
which

which I am not with equal attachment and
refpect, my Lord,

> Your moft humble, &c.

Rome, 3d Jan. 1754.

LETTER LVIII.

TO THE BEARER OF THE HOLY STANDARD OF THE REPUBLICK OF SAINT MARINO.

My dearest Friend,

ALTHOUGH you are only the little
Sovereign of a very little ftate, you
have a foul which puts you on a level with
the greateft Princes. It is not the extent
of Empires which conftitutes the merit of
Emperours. A father of a family may have
great virtue, and a chief Magiftrate of St.
Marino great reputation.

I find nothing fo delightful as being at
the head of a little Diftrict, fcarce perceivable in the map, where neither war nor
difcord are known, and where there are no
ftorms but when the fky is darkened ;——
where there is no ambition, except that of
fupporting one's felf in filence and medio-

crity;—where all property feems to be in common, from the cuftom of every one's being ready to affift his neighbour.

Oh how that little nook of earth pleafes me! How happy to live there! Not in the midft of thofe tumults which diftract great cities; nor in the midft of the great, who opprefs the fmall; nor in the fcenes of pomp, which corrupt the heart and dazzle the eyes. It is a place where I would willingly pitch my tabernacle, and where, from the friendfhip I have for you, my heart has long fixed its abode. There cannot be a greater burthen than fovereignty; but your's is fo light, that it leaves your movements free; efpecially when it is compared with thofe monarchies which the Sovereign cannot govern without multiplying himfelf, and having eyes every where.

Every thing confpires againft a Prince who is at the head of a great kingdom. They who are about him feek to deceive him, at the very time when he perfuades himfelf that they are paying him their court. If he is debauched, they flatter
him

him in his vices; if he is pious, they play the hypocrites, and put on the mask of Religion; if he is cruel, they say he is juft, and he never hears the truth.

He muft often defcend into his own heart to feek it; but, alas! how is he to be pitied, if he does not find it there! Hiftory would not be filled with the reigns of fo many bad Princes, if they had not loved to live at a diftance from truth. Truth is the only fafe friend of Kings, when they will hearken to it; but they often deceive themfelves, looking upon it as an importunate Monitor, that fhould be kept at a diftance, or punifhed for its in-trufion.

As for my part, who have loved it from my infancy, I think that I fhall always love it, tho' it fhould fay the fevereft things. Truths are like bitter medicines, which difpleafe the palate, but reftore our health. Truth is certainly better known at St. Ma-rino than any where elfe—it is feen only obliquely at great courts, but you look it full in the face, and embrace it with the affection of a friend.

M 3

I will

I will not fend you the book you want to fee'—it .is an ill-formed production, badly tranflated from the French, and abounds with herefies againft Morality and found doctrine. It fpeaks, neverthelefs, of *Humanity*; for now-a-days that is the plaufible phrafe, which is fubftituted in the room of *Charity*; becaufe Humanity is but a *Pagan* virtue, and Charity is a Chriftian one. The modern Philofophy is fond of breaking off all connection to Chriftianity, and thereby fhows to the eye of Reafon that it prefers what is defective.

The ancient Philofophers, who were not enlightened by Faith, and had not the advantage of knowing the true God, wifhed for a revelation ; while the modern reject that which they cannot miftake : but in fo doing they betray themfelves ; for if they had a right turn of mind and a pure heart, and were as *humane* as they pretend to be, they would receive with up-lifted hands a Religion which condemns even vicious inclinations, which exprefsly commands the love of our neighbour, and promifeth an eter-

nal

nal recompenfe to all thofe who have afiift-
ed their Brethren, who have been faithful
to their God, their King, and their Country. If we are virtuous, we cannot be averfe
from a Religion which preaches and en-
joins nothing but Virtue.

When I fee the words *legiflation*, *patriotifm*, *bumanity*, conftantly flowing from the
pens of thofe Writers who anathematife
Chriftianity, I fay without any apprehenfion of deceiving myfelf, " Thefe men
" mock the Publick, and inwardly have
" neither Patriotifm nor Humanity." From
the abundance of the heart the mouth
fpeaketh: but fuch men only eftablifh this
general rule, by their being an exception
to it.

Did I think that I had fufficient ftrength
to combat the modern Philofophers, 'tis
in this manner I would make the attack.
They might exclaim againft my arguments, becaufe I fhould prefs them clofely;
but they fhould have no reafon to complain of my fupercilioufnefs. I would fpeak
to them as the tendereft friend, equally
zealous for their good, as for my own; as

a candid and impartial Authour, who would acknowledge thir abilities, and do juſtice to the excellence of their genius.—I am ſo preſumptuous as to believe that they would have eſteemed me, although their antagoniſt.

I cannot execute this deſign, becauſe here I do not enjoy that happy tranquillity which you are in poſſeſſion of at Saint Marino :—there you live in a ſtate of happy leiſure and repoſe, which emulates the condition of the bleſſed.

However, this tranquillity muſt be fatal to the Sciences and the *Belles Lettres* ; for in the immenſe catalogue of celebrated Writers, I do not ſee any of the natives of Saint Marino diſtinguiſhed for their literature. I adviſe you to ſpur up your ſubjects while you are in place ; but make haſte ; for it is not of your kingdom that it is ſaid, *It ſhall have no end.* There is genius in your country, and it wants only to be rouſed.

I have written to you a letter as large as your ſtate, eſpecially if you attend to the heart which dictates it, and in which you

often

often occupy **a very** confiderable place. Thus do they write and love, who have been together at College.   Adieu!

LETTER LIX.

TO COUNT ***.

I WAS of opinion, that you fhould not begin the ftudy of Mathematicks, till you were, my dear friend, confirmed in the principles of Religion.   I was afraid that, by applying yourfelf to a fcience which will admit nothing but what is de-monftrative, you would fall into the common errours of Mathematicians, who think of making our myfteries fubmit to demon-ftration.   The Mathematicks, extenfive as they are, are very limited, when we think of what relates to God.   All the lines that can be drawn upon earth, all the points that can be made, are but infinitely fmall

M 5   in

in comparifon of that immenfe Being, who neither admits parallel nor proportion.

Mathematicks will enable you to think juftly. Without them, there is a certain method wanting which is neceffary to rectify our thoughts, to arrange our ideas, and to determine our judgements aright. It is eafy to perceive in reading a book, even of morality, whether the Authour be a Mathematician or not. I am feldom deceived in this obfervation. The famous French Metaphyfician would not have compofed *The Enquiry after Truth* *, nor the famous Leibnitz his *Theodicée*, if they had not been Mathematicians. We perceive in their productions that geometrical order which brings their reafonings into fmall compafs, while it gives them energy and method.

Order is delightful; there is nothing in nature but what is ftamped with it, and without it there could be no harmony. We may likewife fay, that the Mathematicks are an univerfal fcience which connects all the reft, and difplays them in their happieft relations.

The

* Mallebranche.

The Mathematician is fure, at the firft glance, accurately to analyfe and unravel a fubject or propofition; but a man who does not underftand this fcience, fees only in a vague, and almoft always in an imper-fect, manner.

Apply yourfelf then to this great branch of knowledge, fo worthy of our curiofity, and fo neceffary to the ufes of life; but not in fuch a degree as to throw you into abfence:—endeavour to be always recol-lected, whatever are your ftudies.

If I was as young as you, and had your leifure, I would acquire a more extenfive knowledge of Geometry. I have always cherifhed that fcience with a particular predilection. My turn of mind made me feek with avidity every thing that was me-thodical; and I pay but little refpect to thofe works which are only exercifes of the imagination.

We have three principal Sciences, which I compare to the three effential parts of the human compofition:——Theology, which, by its fpirituality, refembles our foul; the Mathematicks, which by their

combi-

combination and juftnefs, exprefs our reafon; and Natural Philofophy, which, by its
mechanical operations, denotes our bodies:
and thefe three Sciences (which ought to
maintain a perfect harmony) while they
keep within their proper fphere, neceffarily elevate us towards their Authour, the
fource and fullnefs of all light.

I formerly undertook a work, during
my refidence at Afcoli, the intention of
which was to fhow the perfect agreement
between all the Sciences. I pointed out
their fource, their end, and their relations;
but the exercifes of the Cloifter, and the
Lectures I was obliged to give, prevented
its being finifhed. I ftill have fome fragments, which I fhall fearch for among my
papers, and you may read them, if you
think they can amufe you. There are fome
ideas, and fome views; but it is only a
fketch, which muft be filled up by the
Reader, and you are perfectly capable of
the tafk.

Philofophy without Geometry, is like
medicine without chemiftry. The greater
number of modern Philofophers reafon in-
conclufively,

conclufively, only becaufe they are unac-
quainted with Geometry.   They miftake
fophifms for truths ; and though the principles they lay down may be true, the con-
clufions they deduce from them are falfe.

Study alone will not make a learned
man, nor a knowledge of the fciences a
Philofopher.   But we live in an age where
great words impofe, and where men think
themfelves to be eminent geniufes, if they
only contrive a fet of fingular opinions.
Diftruft thofe Writers who employ themfelves rather about the ftyle than the matter, and who hazard every thing for the
fake of furprifing.

I fhall fend you, by the firft opportunity, a work upon Trigonometry ; and if it
is neceffary, I will prove to you geometri-
cally, that is to fay, to a demonftration,
that I am always your beft friend.

ROME, 22d June, 1753.

L E T-

LETTER LX.

TO A FRIAR OF THE MINOR CONVENTUALS.

YOU are miftaken in thinking, my Reverend Father, that I take no part in our general Chapters. I feel a warm intereft in them; not like an ambitious man who defires to obtain promotion, but as a friend of our Order, who wifheth ardently that Pity and Science may there hold the firft rank. A Superior who is only learned may do much harm; and he who is only a devotee may do much more. It is a moft judicious reflection of St. Therefa, *that there is no refource, where there is no underftanding.* Befides Science and Piety, a Superior ought to be endowed with a fpirit of wifdom and difcernment; for there is a great deal of difference between teaching and governing. It has been remarked, that all the Writers, even thofe who have given the fineft leffons to Kings have not been fit for adminiftration. Good fenfe is a

furer

furer guide than fine parts, or even genius, to conduct men prudently. They who have too much vivacity, have too many ideas, and are continually changing their refolutions.

I endeavour, with all poffible zeal, to have thofe chofen Superiors who are fitteft for governing, but without any felfifh view or intrigue. I wifh for no other empire but my Cell, and even there have trouble enough to reftrain my thoughts and imaginations within bounds. Man is fo much the puppet of his paffions, that though always free to act, or to remain inactive, yet he does not always what he would.

What you defire fhall be propofed in the next Affembly ; and I prefume as far as one can anfwer for a multitude of opinions and different fpirits, that they will agree to it. Truth ought naturally to draw all men after it ; but it prefents itfelf under fo many different afpects, that every one judges according to his own eyes ;— the view varies according to our notions, and according to our interefts.

Be

Be convinced that I am, as I have been, always ready to oblige you, and always your good friend and fervant.

LETTER LXI.

TO CARDINAL SPINELLI.

MOST EMINENT,

YOUR Eminency may be fure that the book will be approved as it deferves. Whatever fome people, who think themfelves infpired, may fay, it contains nothing but what is ftrictly orthodox and eafily practicable. If Pharifaical zeal was allowed to govern, we fhould very foon have nothing in the Church but trifling ceremony; and Religion, which is fo beautiful and fublime, would become a round of fuperftitions.

People generally love thofe things which do not tend to reform the heart; and are pleafed with growing old without rooting out bad habits, believing a few prayers repeated in hafte fufficient to carry them to Heaven.

It

It is not aftonifhing that the world fhould feduce us; but it is fuprifing that men who fet themfelves up to oppofe its maxims, do not preferve the fouls of the people from this feduction. Pharifees have lived in all ages, and will continue to the end of the world. They build whitened fepulchres, inftead of erecting temples to the Eternal; and they lull the Faithful afleep, by amufing them with ceremonials, which neither influence the heart nor underftanding.

It were to be wifhed that all the world faw with the fame eyes as your Eminency. What a reformation of abufes! What abfurd ufages fuppreffed! When the Paftor nourifheth himfelf with the Holy Scripture, the Councils, and the Fathers, there is no danger of his Diocefe becoming fuperftitious. Muratori faid, that *trifling practices of devotion for the moft part refemble the compofitions for taking out ftains, which leffen the fpot only in appearance, but, in fact, make it larger.*

Although loaded with bufinefs, I will prove to you, my Lord, by charging myfelf

felf with whatever commands you pleafe to lay upon me, that I will never refufe the happinefs of convincing you of the profound refpect with which I am, &c.

Rome, 3d July, 1752.

LETTER LXII.

TO THE ABBE LAMI.

I DO not know how I fhall be able to recollect myfelf in the midft of the diforders which reign in my Cell and in my head.—Every thing is there pell-mell—one muft write to a methodical Authour like you, to unravel fuch a chaos.

If you had characterifed the poetick genius of each nation, your laft letter would have been a mafter-piece. The Italians are not fuch Poets as the Englifh, nor the Germans fuch as the French. They refemble each other in principles, but they differ in fervency and enthufiafm. The German poefy is a fire which fhines; the French, a fire that fparkles; the Italian, a fire that burns;

burns ; and the Englifh, a fire that blackens.

We accumulate too many images in our pieces in verfe ; and were we lefs prodigal of them, they would make a more lively impreffion. Nothing awakens the Reader better than furprife ; and that cannot happen when thofe things are too often multiplied which produce this effect.

Happy the fober fpirit, which in Poetry, as in Profe, is dedicately fparing in epifodes and defcriptions ! I foon grow tired in a garden in which I fee cafcades and fhrubberies wherever I turn my eyes ; but am charmed with groves and pieces of water difcovered by chance. Violets appear infinitely more beautiful, when feen only by halves, peeping from under a thick foliage. A flower withdrawing from the view excites our curiofity.

Their is nothing beautiful but by comparifon. If every thing was equally magnificent, the eye would foon grow tired with continued admiration. Nature, which ought to be the model of all Writers, varies her objects fo as never to fatigue the fight :

fight: the richeft meadows are found in the neighbourhood of the fimpleft valley; and frequently a charming river at the fide of a gloomy hill.

Repeat thefe leffons, my dear Abbé, to correct our Poets, if poffible, of their pro-fufion of beauties, which refemble heaps of gold piled up without either order or tafte. Your detached fheets are admired as much as your genius; and when a Jour-nalift has acquired this double fame, he may talk like a Mafter, with a certainty of being attended to.

When I was a young Scholar, I loft one of my companions, to whom fympathy had ftrongly united me. Alas! after having taken many folitary walks together, and made many reflections upon things which at that time we knew not, but wifhed to know, he died; and I thought I could not find a better way of affuaging my forrows, than by addreffing fome verfes to him, from a conviction which I then had, and ftill have, that when we appear to die, we only change one life for another.

I dwelt

I dwelt principally upon his candour and piety, for he was a model of virtue. But the fault of this eulogium, as I was made to obferve, was its being overloaded with defcription. I introduced all the beauties of the country, and did not give my Reader time to breathe. It was a tree choaked with leaves and branches, where there was no fruit to be feen.

From that time I never attempted to compofe verfes. I contented myfelf with reading the Poets, and applying myfelf to know their faults and their beauties. All that vexed me was, that my Poem, being fo full of errours, would not defcend to pofterity, and that my friend on every account deferved the honour of being immortalized.

He will never be effaced from my heart: and thus it is that true friends have a refource in fentiment, when they have not fufficient genius to perpetuate the memory of their affections.——This is my pofition in refpect to you. Withdraw your attention from thefe thoughts of mine, to fix it upon the attachment I have vowed to you, and you will find that if I am not a good fpeaker, I am at leaft a good friend and a good fervant. Put me to the proof.

ROME, 10th Dec. 1755.

LETTER LXIII.

TO BARON KRONECH, A GERMAN.

I DO not know, Sir, whether I fhould admire moft your genius or agreeable manners. Nothing can prove better than your example, how eminently the Germans are endowed with the neceffary qualities for forming friendfhips. All thofe with whom I am acquainted, are perfons of the moft amiable difpofition.

If you continue to employ yourfelf ufe-fully, you will do honour to your nation, and to all thofe who have known you. I congratulate myfelf that an accident pro-cured me the pleafure of your agreeable converfation. I have always been a gainer by being communicative; for I have met

with

with people who have merited the ſtrong-
eſt attachment, or who have needed advice and aſſiſtance.

It is ſo agreeable to oblige, that when
we are actuated by that motive, we cannot make too great advances to thoſe that
fall in our way. I could wiſh not to finiſh
this letter, from the deſire I have to entertain you; but I muſt attend prayers, and
my uſual employments and beſides am
afraid of tiring you. Receive, then, without ceremony, the vows which I put up
that I may ſee you again, and that I may
repeat how much I have the honour to be

Your's, &c.

L E T-

LETTER LXIV.

TO MONS. DE LA BRUYERE,

CHARGED WITH THE AFFAIRS OF FRANCE AT THE COURT OF ROME.

SIR,

I CALLED at your houfe, with a defign to fteal at leaft one hour of your time, with a certainty of improving by it; but I could not penetrate into that precious clofet, from whence you correfpond with that of Verfailles in a manner fo honourable to yourfelf, and advantageous for your amiable nation.

I retired very fpeedily, as I have no politicks, but that of taking care to be engaged in none; I returned faying to myfelf, that I ought not to appear again at your houfe unlefs I am fent for.

Yet, if I knew the hour you dedicate to your good Friends, the *Belles-Lettres*, I would anxioufly endeavour to approach you. Something would iffue from your excellent memory and brilliant imagina-

tion,

tion, which would embellish mine, and
serve to diftinguish me in fociety.

I always regret having heard but half
the reading of a certain manufcript, where
Rome, fhown as fhe is, moft amply fatis-
fies the curiofity. There the flowers are
mixed with the fruit, and it is the moft
agreeable bafket which can be prefented to
people of tafte. My foul is impatient to
hear the reft. I know you are too obliging
not to fatisfy her defire.

You could not have chofen a happier
epoch than the reign of Benedict XIV. to
paint Rome to advantage. It feems as if he
revived this City in the eyes of Foreigners,
and that the Sciences refume frefh luftre
to pay their court to him: fo true it is,
that a Monarch only is wanted to give
life and motion even to things that are inanimate.

If by great accident there happens to be
one hour with which you are embarraffed,
fend for Ganganelli, and he will prove to
you, that there is neither ftudy, bufinefs,
nor vifit, which can detain him, when he

is called upon to prove the zeal with which he has the honour to be, &c.

ROME, 2d March, 1753.

LETTER LXV.

TO THE SAME

INDEED you are too generous, when you would give me three hours of your time, and leave them to my own choice. To-morrow, then, since you allow me, I will go and enjoy the benefit of your kindnefs. It would be in vain to whifper to my Genius, to deck herfelf out for this interview with all the elegance fhe is miftrefs of; for fhe muft be content with admiring you in filence. Timidity, with a confcioufnefs of poffeffing but few or trifling accomplifhments, will hinder her from appearing to the leaft advantage before you. You muft therefore expect to be at the whole expence of the entertainment yourfelf; and no one but you, who are as

m odeft

modeſt as you are well informed, will re-
pine at it.

Notwithſtanding all the pleaſure I ſhall
have in waiting on you, I ſhould ſtill have
more, if the Duke de Nivernois is yet with
you, whoſe ſoul and genius is univerſally
admired. He is one who is only learned
with the learned, and whoſe Science, if
we may uſe the expreſſion, is interwoven
with Roſes and Jeſſamine.

I will communicate to you a production
of one of our young Monks, which will
convince you that there is not only learning, but likewiſe genius to be met with in
the Cloiſter, when talents are exerciſed as
if they were encouraged. Plants that have
been thought barren, have ſometimes produced moſt excellent fruit.

I have the honour, &c.

ROME, 3d March. 1753.

LETTER LXVI.

TO CARDINAL QUIRINI, BISHOP OF BRESCIA.

MOST EMINENT,

YOUR Eminency does me too much honour, and has too good an opinion of my weak abilities, when you deign to afk me how Theology fhould be ftudied and taught.

Formerly there was only one way of unfolding that fublime Science, which having its fource in God himfelf, fpreads in the midft of the Church like a majeftick and copious river ; and that was called the *Pofitive*.

From the refpect which was paid to the facred Doctrines of the Holy Scriptures, the Councils, and the Fathers, the Profeffors of Theology, were undoubtedly content to place morals and the evangelical opinions, in their greateft fimplicity, before the eyes of the ftudents. Thus the Commandments of God were propofed
formerly

formerly to the Jews without a commentary, and they treafured them up in their
hearts and memories, as what ought principally to engage them, and be the means
of their happinefs.

The Church, although feated upon the
Holy Mountain whofe foundations are
eternal, has been always agitated by tempefts, and from time to time has feen rebel-
lious children fpringing from her bowels,
who had learned the delufions of Sophi-
ftry; and it was their artful language which
obliged the Defenders of the Faith to af-
fume the method of fyllogifm.

All the world knows the time when certain Teachers were obliged to arm themfelves with Enthymemes and Syllogifms,
to drive thofe Hereticks from their laft en-
trenchments, who cavilled at the mean-
ings of the Scripture, and at all its terms.

Thomas, that Angel of the Schools, and
Scotus, that fubtle Doctor, thought they
muft make ufe of the fame form; and
their method, fupported by their fhining
reputation, infenfibly prevailed in the Uni-
verfities.

N 3   But

But as every thing commonly degene-
rates, it was not poffible to keep the *pofitive* Theology in ufe ; and the manner of
teaching in the Schools, which thence got
the name of *fcholaftick*, ran too often upon
words and diftinctions. They perplexed
every thing, from their follicitude to clear
up every thing, and often replied to nothing, from their defire to anfwer all.

Befides that this wrangling only fuited
Philofophy, it had the appearance of rendering the moft certain things problema-
tical ; and this was the more unhappy, as
they agitated fome ridiculous queftions,
and fplit upon myfteries, whofe fublimity
and depth ought to have ftopped every
man of reflection.

However, as the Scholaftick method
had the advantage of affifting the memory,
by giving form to reafonings ; and the
abufe with which it is reproached, never
darkened the holy truths, whofe reign is as
lafting as God himfelf, it was thought
proper ftill to preferve it.

I have always thought, my Lord, that
the Scholaftick manner modified, as it is
taught

taught at the Sapienza in Rome, and in the firſt Schools of the Chriſtian world, might ſubſiſt without enervating morals, or altering doctrines, provided the Profeſſors be men of ſound underſtanding, and not apt to miſtake ſimple opinions for articles of Faith.

Nothing more dangerous than to give as a matter of Faith, what is only a matter of opinion; and to confound a pious belief with a thing which is revealed. The true Theologiſt employs only real and ſolid diſtinctions, and draws no conſequences but from clear and preciſe principles.

A truth is never better eſtabliſhed than by the univerſal approbation of all the Churches, which is a circumſtance the greater part of modern Theologians do not ſufficiently attend to. The tenets of the Euchariſt never appeared more ſolidly eſtabliſhed, than when the doctrines on that ſubject among the Roman Catholicks and the Greek Schiſmaticks were ſhown to be ſo ſimilar.

Theology

Theology, to be folid and fhining, that is to fay, to preferve its moft effential attributes, needs only a clear and fimple expofition of all the articles of the Faith, and then it will appear fupported by all its proofs, and all its authorities.

If Theologians would eftablifh, for example, the truth of the myftery of the Incarnation, they muft fhow that God, who could not act but for himfelf, had in view at the creation of the world, the Eternal Word by whom the world was made ; and *that in forming Adam*, as Tertullian fays, *he traced out the lineaments of Jefus Chrift*. This is conformable to the doctrine of St. Paul, who declares in the moft exprefs manner, that all exifts in the Divine Mediator, and fubfifts only by him : *Omnia per ipfum & in ipfo conftant*.

They prove afterwards by the types and the prophefies, whofe authenticity they fhow, that the Incarnation is their object, and that there is nothing in thefe holy books which does not relate to it, directly or indirectly : then they fhow the time and the place where this ineffable myftery was accomplifhed, accomplished, examining the character of the signs which accompanied it, the witnesses which attested it, the wonders which followed it, and display all the traditions upon that subject.

They next demonstrate the authority of the Fathers of the Church, point out the force of their reasonings, the sublimity of their comparisons; and employ the Scholastick method to unravel the sophistries of heresiarchs, to combat and conquer them with their own weapons.

Thus Positive theology resembles a magnificent garden, and the Scholastick method of reasoning is a hedge stuck with thorns, to prevent noxious animals from getting in and ravaging it.

If I taught only the Scholastick method when I was Lecturer in Theology, it was because, being of the same brotherhood with Scorus, I could not decline teaching after his method. An individual cannot change the mode of instruction in an Order of which he is a member, but with an ill grace; it might be often attended with bad consequences—not that we should servilely embrace fantastical opinions.

N 5

For

For you, my Lord, who in quality of Bifhop, have an inconteftible right to prefcribe the method of teaching, and give it what form you pleafe, I beg of you to recommend to your Theologians to ufe the Scholaftick mode with difcretion, for fear of enervating Theology.

I believe your views would be anfwered, if they were to draw from the fources, inftead of fimply copying from the manufcript theologies; and if they would be content to explain the doctrines of the Church without giving into difputes, or party fpirit.

This fpirit is the more dangerous, my Lord, as they then fubftitute their own opinions for eternal truths, which every one ought to refpect; and enter into altercations, which, under pretence of fupporting the caufe of God, extinguifh charity.

Do not permit them to fupport free will, by denying the almighty power of Grace; nor by enhancing the value of that ineftimable and entirely free gift, to deftroy liberty; nor from too great refpect for the Saints, to forget what they owe

I   to

to Jefus Chrift. Theological truths are fo clofely connected, that they may all be confidered as one; and there are fome covered with a myfterious veil, which it is impoffible to draw afide.

The great fault of fome Theologians is a defire to explain every thing, and not knowing where to ftop. The Apoftle has told us, for example, in fpeaking of Heaven, *that eye hath not feen, nor ear heard what God hath referved for his Saints*; and yet they give us a defcription of Paradife as if they had juft returned from thence. They affign ranks to the Chofen, and would almoft cry out " Herefy !" againft the men who fhould dare to contradict them. The true Theologian ftops where he fhould; and when a thing has not been revealed, or the church has not pronounced upon it, he does not take upon him to decide. There will always be an impenetrable cloud between God and man, till the moment of eternity.

The types ceafed with the Old Law, to give place to reality; but the evidence is not to be found till after death; fuch is

the

the œconomy of Religion. It were to be wifhed, my Lord, that in fpeaking of God they would always pronounce his name with a holy fervour; not as a Being whom they read, but as a Spirit whofe immenfe perfections excite the greateft refpect and admiration. Thus, inftead of faying that God would be unjuft, God would be a liar, God would not be all-powerful, if fuch and fuch things happened; they fhould take care that no fuch injurious expreffions be joined to that name. Let us be content to anfwer with St. Paul; "Can "there be any injuftice in God? God for-" bid:" *Numquid iniquitas apud Deum? Abfit.*

The name of God is fo aweful and holy, that it fhould never be introduced into human compofitions or debates. It is not enough that man may exercife his talents upon the phenomena of Nature, that he may difpute about the elements and their effects, without making God himfelf the fubject of his argument?

This has rendered Theology ridiculous in the eyes of Freethinkers, and has perhaps

haps taught them to ufe the Almighty's name in all their objections and their far-cafm—For how can Theology, which is the difplay of the wifdom of Providence, and the attributes of an Infinite Being, who is all-excellent and all powerful, appear to be a trifling fcience, except from its being prefented without dignity? Shall the nature of a grain of fand that the wind fporteth with at pleafure, of an infect that is trod under foot, of the earth itfelf which is perifhable, be ftudied before the knowledge of God himfelf? that God from whom we have our being, in whom we live and move, before whom the fea is but a drop of water, the mountains a point, and the whole univerfe an atom?

It is with the grandeur of the Immenfe and Supreme Being, that the Theologian fhould begin his courfe of Theology. After having demonftrated his abfolute neceffary exiftence, and that it is neceffarily eternal; after having fought for the creation of fpirits even in his bofom; after having proved that all flows from him as

its

its firſt principle ; that all breathes in him as its centre ; that all returns to him as its end ; he ſhould then diſplay his immenſe wiſdom, and his infinite goodneſs, from whence reſults Revelation, and the worſhip it has ordained.

Then the natural law, the written law, and the law of Grace, ſhould appear each in their pre-eminence, and according to the order of Chronology. He ſhould next demonſtrate how God was always worſhipped by a ſmall number in ſpirit and in truth ; how the Church annihilated the Synagogue, and from age to age cut off thoſe rebels who would have corrupted its morals and opinions ; and how, always powerful in words and works, it was ſupported by learned Teachers, and preſerved its purity amidſt the moſt dreadful ſcandals and cruel diviſions.

It is neceſſary that thoſe who ſtudy Theology ſhould be edified by what is taught them, and not be amuſed by falſe glimmerings, more capable of dazzling than illuminating them. Let them be led to the pureſt ſouɾce, under the guidance of

St.

St. Auguftine and St. Thomas, and fhun
with care whatever has the appearance of
novelty—let them be infpired with a fpirit of evangelical toleration, with a tendernefs even for thofe who combat the Faith,
and be impreffed with the fpirit of Jefus
Chrift, which is not that of harfhnefs or
of tyranny.

It is not by invectives againft hereticks,
nor by giving vent to a bitter zeal againft
unbelievers, that they are to be led back
into the way of truth; but by manifefting
a fincere defire for their converfion, and
by fpeaking of them in the moft affectionate terms, even at the time when their fo-
phiftries are to be expofed.

It is neceffary that the Profeffors of
Theology fhould oppofe the Pagan Theologians to the Chriftian, as the fureft
means of overturning their Mythology,
covering their ancient fuperftitions with
perpetual ridicule, and raifing the doctrines
of the Incarnate Word on their ruins.

It is yet more neceffary that thefe Profeffors be not fyftematical. They fhould
depend upon the Church, the Scriptnres,

and

and Tradition, when they teach eternal Truths; becaufe they are then deputed by the body of Paſtors to teach in their name, and to exercife their power,

Would to God they had faithfully followed this method; The Church would not have feen the moſt afflicting and obſtinate difputes arife in her bofom, paſſion take place of charity, and the hatred of the Teachers produce the moſt fatal effects.

Hence it follows, my Lord, that your Eminency cannot be too attentive in appointing moderate men as Theologians, from the apprehenfion that bitter zeal may do more harm than good. The fpirit of the Gofpel is a fpirit of peace, and it is not right that they who do preach it fhould be turbulent.

If I durſt, my Lord, I would beg your Eminency to compofe a body of Theology which fhould be the eſtabliſhed leſſon of your Diocefe, and would certainly be adopted by a number of Biſhops. The liberty of the Schools fhould only be allowed in different queſtions; becaufe there is only one Baptifm and one Faith.

Theology

Theology fhould not be employed to exercife the genius of young people, but to enlighten them, and to raife them up, even to Him who is the fullnefs and fource of all light.

It will be proper to provide the Scholars with the beft books relative to the doc- trines which are taught them. The beft way of ftudying Religion, is to make them- felves well acquainted with the Holy Scrip- tures, the Councils, and the Fathers. Such a courfe of ftudy will prevent them from ftraying into the paths of errour, and teach them to fpeak of Chriftianity in a manner worthy of the fubject.

I have nothing further to add, my Lord, but that a Profeffor of Theology fhould be equally learned and pious. Eternal truths fhould, as far as it is poffible, be only heard from lips that are holy. There will refult from thence a bleffing from Heaven upon the Mafter, the Scholars, and an odour of life upon the whole Diocefe. Italy has always had Theologians, whofe life kept pace with the purity of their doctrine.

Excufe

Excuse my temerity, my Lord, which would have been unpardonable, if your Eminency had not commanded me to give you my opinion.

I submit it wholly to your judgement, having the honour to be, with the most perfect obedience, and the profoundest respect, &c.

ROME, 21st May, 1753.

LETTER LXVII.

TO THE COUNT DE BIELK, A SENATOR OF ROME.

I WILL wait upon your most illustrious Lordship, as soon as possibly I can, to examine the manuscript you did me the favour to mention. There is no place where a Monk can be more at his ease, than with your Excellency. He there finds delicious retirement, exquisite books, and your amiable conversation. There is nothing so agreeable in the commerce of life,

as

as that philofophick Liberty which fhakes off fervitude, elevates itfelf above grandeur, acts without conftraint, and is governed by no rule but duty.

And yet you tell me that you are not happy. Alas! what is it you want to make you fo? Thofe haughty Romans, who formerly inhabited the Capitol where you refide, notwithftanding their reputation and philofophy, poffeffed not your tranquillity: — they lived in the midft of tempefts, and you are in the centre of peace — they were always in war, and Rome is now the city of which the Prophet fpeaks, *whofe borders were peace: Qui pofuit fines fuos pacem.*

It is neither in riches nor in buftle that we can be happy; but in a well chofen fociety of books and friends. We are undone if humour or caprice gets poffeffion of us—they are our greateft enemies.

Your Excellency has fuch refources in your own mind, that you ought never to complain of liftleffnefs. For my part, I have only a fort of dictionary knowledge of that evil. But if it was at any time to intrude into my Cell, I fhould foon find a remedy

remedy for it: I would come and profit by your knowledge, and often repeat to you the fentiments of refpect and efteem with which I am, &c.

CONVENT of the HOLY APOSTLES.

LETTER LXVIII.

TO COUNT ***.

WELL, my dear friend, what are you doing? It is a long time fince I faw you; I certainly do not deferve to be deprived of that pleafure. You know that I willingly quit my pen, my employment, and my books, when you come to fee me.

They who come to vifit us, have no occafion for our ftudies nor our bufinefs; and that is what very few reclufes think of. They are only employed about themfelves or their intereft, when you meet them, without reflecting that they ought

to

to dedicate themfelves entirely to thofe who come to feek them.

I have always made it a law to receive every perfon well who honours me with a vifit, even the man who comes to importune me—it is fufficient that he is my · neighbour. Now judge after this, if you will be well received.

It is almoft eighteen days fince I faw the little Abbé. I am afraid, but I dare not tell you that—The art of being filent is a great virtue :—happy they who fay nothing but what they ought to fpeak! Accuftom yourfelf to be fecret, without affecting difcretion— a myfterious man is infufferable in fociety; and it requires little fagacity eafily to penetrate the views of him who always appears to keep his mind to himfelf.

I am not referved, but I make nobody my confidant, with regard either to my correfpondents or relations. Never employ fineffe ; it is a wretched refource, incompatible with probity, and eafily difcovered.

I have been already told who the Lady is that is defigned for you; and from the

picture

picture which has been given of her, as a person who has neither falfe devotion, pretended modefty, nor fantaftical humours, I think fhe will fuit you.

I will tell you more when we meet; but let it be foon, to-morrow, to-day, inftantly. I am without referve your fervant and beft friend, &c.

LETTER LXIX.

TO R. P. CONCINA, A DOMINICAN.

IT is undoubtedly very ftrange, my Reverend Father, that in an age fo enlightened there fhould be Cafuifts to teach the abominations which you combat. They who find your zeal too bitter, do not know what Religion exacts, when morals and opinions are attacked. In fuch a cafe 'tis right to fay to you, *Clama, ne ceffes* *.

If the Church had never exclaimed with a loud voice, every fort of errour would have

* Cry without ceafing.

have ſtolen imperceptibly upon her; but
whenever a heterodox or relaxed opinion
ſtarted up, immediately the ſacred trumpet
was ſounded, that Paſtors might watch inceſſantly to ſtop the ſource of the evil.

Your work gave me a moſt ſenſible pleaſure. I found in it that holy zeal which
characteriſes the Fathers of the Church.   I
would very willingly come to ſee you; but
your employments, like mine, prevent me
from gratifying the inclination I ſhould
have to aſſure you verbally of the reſpectful conſideration with which I have the honour to be, &c.

ROME, 7th March, 1753.

LETTER LXX.

TO CARDINAL GENTILI.

MOST EMINENT,

I WILL attend exactly at the hour your
Eminency hath appointed, being jea-
lous of proving, upon every occaſion, how
much your orders are reſpectable in my
ſight.

fight. It will be impoffible for me to bring
the writing you mention, as it is not finifhed ; but I will endeavour to fupply what
is wanting from my memory. Sometimes
it ferves me very well. I am with the pro-
foundeft refpect,

Your Eminency's, &c.

ROME, 7th March 1752.

LETTER LXXI.

TO MONSIGNOR ZALUSKI, GRAND REFFE-RENDARY OF POLAND.

MY LORD,

I HAVE fruitlefly fearched for the
book you afk of me : it is neither in
our library, nor in all Rome. It will require a fagacity equal to your own to be
able to difcover it: for what work is there
which you have not dragged from its con-
cealment ? There is not a book in the world
which does not owe you homage, or can
efcape your fearch.

You

You will perpetuate the honour which the Polifh nation hath acquired at all times, by fignalizing your uncommon erudition. We fhall never forget Copernicus for Natural Philofophy, Hofius for Theology, Zalufki for Hiftory, Zamoifki for the *Belles-Lettres*, the Fathers of the Pious Schools for learning, and Sobiefki for the art of war.

The library which you have made public, in concert with your illuftrious brother the Bifhop of Cracow, is filled with Polifh Writers who diftinguifh themfelves on every fubject. It is a pity fo celebrated a Republick fhould not encourage a love of fcience among its fubjects, and that the fpirit fo natural to your worthy countrymen fhould remain uncultivated.

The wars, of which Poland has been fo often the dreadful theatre, have made a number of Authors mifcarry. They would have penned the productions of their genius with indelible ink, as they have written the proofs of their valour with their own blood.

Vol. I.   O   Circum-

Circumstances almost always determine the fate of men — one stifles his taste for the sciences by turning soldier; another recommends himself by his learning, because he leads a private life; and it is Providence which disposeth all for the best; *fortiter suaviterque disponens omnia.*

I wish, my Lord, that your love of books and sciences would inspire you with a desire to revisit Rome. You came formerly to be instructed—you will come now to give lessons, to receive the respects of all the world, and in particular those of

Your most humble, &c.

ROME, 9th July, 1755.

LETTER LXXII.

TO A MONK, ONE OF HIS FRIENDS, APPOINTED A BISHOP.

AFTER having been an humble Disciple of St. Francis, you are now placed in the rank of the Apostles. It is sufficient to tell you, my dear friend, that you

you ought not to raife yourfelf to dignity,
except to be truely the ferva nt of all; you
ought not to fhine, but by the luftre of
your virtue.

There is not a dignity upon earth fo formidable in the eyes of the Faithful, as that of
a Bifhop. He muft watch night and day
over the **flock** of Jefus Chrift, and think
that he is to anfwer at his tribunal for every
ftray fheep. He muft renew himfelf, that
he **may** not tire—multiply himfelf, that
he **may** be every where—and be alone,
that **he** may ftudy and pray.

There are two things fo effential for
Bifhops, that they cannot deferve the title,
without poffeffing them in **an** eminent
degree - purity, **to** render them like the
Angels themfelves, and which has procured them that name in the Holy Scriptures,
as appears in the firft chapters of the Revelations—and knowledge, which intitles
them to the honour of being called *the
light of the world,* in the Gofpel itfelf. As
men bearing an immaculate character, they
ought not to have their morals in the leaft
fufpected; and are likewife obliged to

preferve

preferve others from corruption ; for which reafon they are called the *falt of the earth*. With refpect to their learning, they ought to be *eyes to the blind, feet to the lame*, and *the light to the world*. It is not fufficient that a Bifhop be virtuous, and confult learned men to know what he fhall do ; he ought to be able to difcern good from evil, and truth from errour, for he is to judge of doctrines and morals ; and if he does not poffefs a talent for judging, he will not have a talent for governing, and will be eafily deceived.

What comforts me is, that you are folidly inftructed, and that you will fee all yourfelf ; which is abfolutely neceffary, that you may not be the dupe of hypocrites or informers.

I do not doubt of your having already meditated ferioufly upon the Epiftle of Paul to Timothy, and of St. Peter to all the Faithful. In the firft, you muft have feen that a Bifhop ought to be irreprehenfible, fober, chafte and peaceable ; that he may not live like thofe Prelates whofe hiftory is exactly that of the rich man
clothed

POPE CLEMENT XIV.   293

clothed in purple and fine linen, and who lived every day in fplendour, but leave Lazarus to die at their gate.

From the fecond you will have learned not to domineer over any Ecclefiaftick under your care; for the fpirit of Jefus Chrift is not a fpirit of dominion, but a fpirit of gentlenefs and humility; fo that a biſhop ought to look upon the Curates as his equals, in the order of Chriſtian charity, though they are not fo in that of the Hierarchy. His houfe ought to be ever open to receive them.

Do not flightly difpenfe with your feldom preaching the word of God, remembering what St. Paul faid, that *he was not fent to baptize, but to preach*. Manage fo, that there be no Sacrament which you do not adminifter from time to time, to ſhow your Diocefans that you devote yourſelf to them in ficknefs or in health, at their births as well as at their deaths.

Above all, vifit regularly the Diocefe which is entrufted to you, and take care that your vifits be not like tempefts which

O 3   infpire

infpire terrour, but like beneficent dews fpreading chearfulnefs and fertility.

If you find by chance any of your af-fiftants who have finned, ftretch over him the cloke of charity, to lead him back to his duty by gentlenefs, and to hide the fcandal as much as poffible. If he has been guilty of a crime, engage him fecretly to quit his fituation, but fecure a retreat for him before he leaves it.

I will not defire you to have a paternal tendernefs for the Monks; That would be to offend you. You owe to them what you now are, and it was at their fchool that you, as well as I, learnt all that we know. Vifit them often with cordiality; it is the way to excite a juft emulation among them, and to make them re-fpected. It is to do honour to one's felf, to honour thofe whofe lives are a continual labour. A general who fhould defpife his officers, would deferve the greateft contempt himfelf.

Do not fuffer the piety of the Faithful to be fed with falfe legends, nor to be oc-cupied in petty obfervances; but teach
them

them to inftruct their flock ; to have re-
courfe conftantly to Jefus Chrift, as our
only Mediator, and to honour the Saints
only in reference to him.   The method of
inftruction is left to you, and you fhould
know what they teach.

Be cautious whom you admit into Orders ; for Italy abounds with fupernume-
rary Priefts, who carry their ignorance and
poverty into foreign nations, debafing the
dignity of the Priefthood, and difhonour-
ing their country.

Give benefices which **have a** charge
of fouls, only to perfons of acknow-
ledged merit, efpecially in learning and
piety; **and** pay attention to him who has
long laboured, **in** preference to one newly
ordained.

Affociate with you for the government
of your Diocefe thofe only who have
grown grey in the Miniftry, and whofe
age, as well as virtue, will give them authority. A Bifhop **is** defpifed who has
only young people for his fociety and
council, becaufe on every occafion they
can influence his judgement. The Pope has

O 4   only

only one Vicar General, and confequently one is fufficient for you.

Let the loweft of your titles be *my Lord*, and thofe of *Father* and *Servant* be much more dear to you; for *the fafhion of this world paffeth away*, and all grandeur with it.

In fine, while in the midft of riches and honours, do not receive more than is necef-fary to fupply your wants, and make you refpected; reflecting, that Saint Paul *kept his body in fubjection,* and that every Chriftian ought to mortify himfelf.

Above all, I fay, refide, and I fay again, refide. A Shepherd, who without reafon keeps at a diftance from his flock, has no right to eat.

Thefe are harfh truths; but as we can-not change them, you muft either fubmit to them, or abdicate.

Let the poor be your friends, your bro-thers, and your companions. You can-not give too much. Alms-giving is one of the moft effential obligations of a Bifhop, and muft be done in houfes, in prifons, in publick places, indeed every-where, to fol-low the fteps of our Divine Saviour, who
never

gmentgment gmentgmentgmentgmentgment=gmentgmentgmentgmentgmentgment >gmentgmentgmentgmentgmentgmentgmentgmentgmentgmentgmentgment POPE CLEMENT XIV. 297

never ceafed during his mortal life to do good. But give with chearfulnefs—*hilarem datorem diligit Deus* *—and give in fuch a manner that you become indigent yourfelf.

I fay nothing to you about your domeftic employments, convinced that you will divide your time between prayer, ftudy, and the government of your Diocefe. A Bifhop never tires of reading the Scriptures and the Fathers, when he knows their value, when he doth not live in diffipation, and is fenfible that a Bifhoprick is a formidable burthen, and not a fecular dignity.

Hear all the world, and make yourfelf popular after the example of our Divine Mafter, who allowed even little children to approach him, and fpoke to them with the greateft goodnefs. Frequently vifit thofe individuals of your Diocefe who have met with any misfortune, that you may be their help and their comfort.

It is an odious thing in a Bifhop to know none but thofe of rank and fortune

O 5

in

* God loveth a chearful giver.

in his Diocefe. The lower people murmur, and with reafon ; for they are often more precious in the fight of God.

If there fhould **be any** difpute among the inhabitants of the **town** where your Bi-fhoprick lies, inftantly become a mediator. A Bifhop fhould know no law-fuits but thofe of other people, and labour to accommodate them.

Examine the Ecclefiafticks yourfelf, who apply for Orders, and take care that they never be afked queftions that are childifh, or foreign to what they ought to know. Take care that your Confeffors obferve the Rules of St. Charles **in the** Tribunal of Penitence.

Do not, on pretence of bufinefs, fall into the habit of going but feldom to your Church. The Publick will not be fatiffied with **fuch** reafons; they defire to be edified ; and who will pray to God, if the Bifhop will not ?

When you have thus filled up the meafure of your time, you will find yourfelf furrounded with a multitude of good **works** at the hour **of death.** You know
that

that they follow us into eternity, while pride, grandeur, and titles, are loft in the darknefs of the grave, and leave a frightful void in the foul. Read often what is faid to the Bifhops defcribed in the Revelations, and tremble.

I believe I have run over all the duties of a Bifhop in this letter—it is your duty to practife them. You have certainly faid to yourfelf, and much better than I can, what I have juft now reminded you of, but you called upon me for my advice.— It proceeds, I fwear to you, from the moft lively friendfhip, and fincere defire to fee you labour effectually toward your own falvation, in labouring for that of others. You are doubly obliged to this, both as a Monk and a Bifhop.

I wait your being inducted, to write to you with more ceremony. Adieu! I embrace you with all my heart.

CONVENT of the HOLY APOSTLES,
      30th May, 1755.

LETTER LXXIII.

TO THE ABBE LAMI.

I AM enchanted with your laſt ſheet. Your criticiſm is accurate, and it is thus you ſhould cenſure. without impatience, caprice, or impartiality, according to the rules of juſtice and taſte. Growing talents have often been diſcouraged by being judged with too much rigour. I do not know any one work, ancient or modern, which will not appear defective, if you are diſpoſed to criticiſe every part of it. Authours have need of the indulgence of Reviewers; and Reviewers themſelves, of the indulgence of the Publick; becauſe there is nothing abſolutely perfect.

I am much obliged to you for the account you give us, from time to time, of French books. Thoſe of the laſt age had more force, but thoſe of the preſent are more pleaſing. It is common enough to have the fine give place to the pretty; it is the diminutive which is derived from

2   the

the fubftantive. Your eulogium of Cardinal Lancé is juftly due to him.   He edifies the whole Church by his fhining virtues, and they are accompanied with an
immenfe variety of knowledge.   I fhould
be delighted, if he lived at Rome ;—I
would endeavour to merit his approbation,
in order to enjoy the benefit of his enlightened underftanding.   He is a pupil
of the Congregation of St. Genevieve in
France, fo renowned for knowledge and
piety, and wore the habit of that Order for
fome time.

LETTER LXXIV.

TO A GENTLEMAN OF TUSCANY.

THE education you propofe giving
your children will be only a varnifh,
if it is not founded upon Religion. There
are fome occafions in the courfe of life,
where probity is not fufficiently ftrong to
refift certain temptations, and where the
foul

foul is debafed, if it is not elevated by the firm belief of Immortality.

It is neceffary for the wifdom and happinefs of man, that he fhould have a view of the Deity from his tendereft infancy as the principle and the end of all things ; and Reafon and Faith fhould tell him, that it is defcending to the rank of beafts to be without either worfhip or law : he fhould be made to know that Truth being one, there can be only one Religion ; and if our belief was not determined by authority, every one would have his own fyftem and his own opinion.

It is not by an attention to trifling ceremonies that you will make your children true Chriftians. Chriftianity is the greateft enemy to Pharifaical zeal and fuperftition. The Church prefcribes duties enough without our endeavouring to multiply them. We too frequently neglect what is precept, to follow what is only advice, becaufe we love rather to hearken to caprice than to reafon ; and becaufe pride and fingularity perfectly agree.

You

You fhould take a great deal of pains to elevate the fouls of your three young people, and to convince them, that the greateft pleafure of man is to reflect, and to be confcious of his exiftence. This is a pleafure fo fublime, and fo worthy of a heavenly fpirit, that I look upon him who knows not this happinefs, as a wretched, or, at leaft, an infenfible being.

The Catechifm is fufficient to teach revealed Truths; but in an age of infidelity, fomething more is wanted than the Alphabet of Religion: You fhould therefore fill your children's minds with thofe pure lights which diffipate the clouds of modern philofophy, and the darknefs of corruption.

A few but folid books will make your children **well**-informed Chriftians. Let them be read lefs with an intention to fix them in the memory, than to grave them on the heart. It is not neceffary to form young people to defend a thefis, but to be obliged, as rational creatures, to convince themfelves of eternal truths.

4

When

When youth have ftudied Religion from its firft principles, they feldom fuffer themfelves to be feduced by fophiftry and impiety, unlefs the heart be entirely corrupted.

You fhould watch carefully to preferve them fpotlefs, not by employing informers and fpies, but by having your ears and your eyes every where to imitate the Deity whom we do not fee, but who feeth over all.

Children fhould not perceive that they are diftrufted and obferved, for that will difcourage them, and make them murmur; they will conceive averfion againft thofe they ought to love, fufpect an evil which they would not have thought of, and feek only to deceive:—Hence it is that all Scholars act only from fear, and are never more pleafed than when at a diftance from their Superiors.

Be lefs the mafter than the friend of your children; and then they will be tranfparent to your eyes, and even tell their faults themfelves. Young folks have a hundred times told me their griefs and

their

their errours, becaufe I always treat them with mildnefs—they will give you the key of their hearts, when they find that you fincerely wifh them well, and that it is a pain to you to reprove them.

There are many reafons which induce me to advife a domeftick education, and there are ftill more which hinder me from perfuading you to it. Domeftick education is commonly the beft calculated to fecure their morals; but it prefents fuch a famenefs, it is fo luke-warm and languid, that it difcourages all emulation: befides, as they are watched too narrowly, they more frequently become hyprocrites than good pupils.

Neverthelefs, if you can find a Preceptor, gentle, patient, fociable, and learned, who can unite condefcenfion with fteadinefs, wifdom with gaiety, temperance with amiablenefs, I fhould defire you to make the tryal; being perfuaded that you will do nothing but in concert with him, and that you will not feek to control him. There are too many Fathers who look upon a Preceptor as a mercenary, and illiberally

think

think **they** are his mafters, becaufe he receives their wages.

Truft your fons only to a man upon whom you can depend as upon yourfelf ; but after you have found fuch a man, do not hefitate to leave them **entirely at his** difpofal. Nothing difgufts **a Tutor fo** much, as diftruft and a diffidence **of his** capacity. Take care what fervants you admit about your children ; it is generally through them that youth are corrupted.

Manage fo as **to** have an amiable fereni-ty conftantly fhining on your face and **in** your eyes, and that every thing be done **as** you would have it, without reftraint **or** fear. Nobody loves a **ftorm ;** but all the world rejoices in fine weather.

Attach pleafures **to every** kind of ftudy which **you** propofe for your fons, by exciting a keen defire of knowledge, and an ardent impatience of ignorance.

Take care that they have **relaxation** from their ftudies, that their memories and judgements may **not** grow tired. When difguft **is** joined with ftudy, they

conceive

conceive an averfion to books, and figh
after idlenefs and fupinenefs.

Inftruct them **by** making them love,
your documents, not by the fear of pu-
nifhments ; and for this purpofe take
care to enliven them by fome little hifto-
ries or fallies, which may awaken attention. I knew a young man at Milan who
became fuch a lover of ftudy, that he
looked upon holidays as neceffary for relaxation, but confidered them as days of
forrow ; his books were his pleafure and
his treafure. It was a good Prieft who by
chearfulnefs, and the refources of his imagination, had infpired him with a love for
works of tafte and learning. He would
have been **one of** the moft learned men in
Europe, **if** death **had** not ftopped him in
his career.

Adapt their ftudies to their **times of life,**
and do **not** think of making them Meta-
phyficians at twelve years **old :** That is
not educating **young** people, **but** teaching
words to parrots.

Learning is like food. The ftomach
of a child requires light nourifhment ; and
it

it is only by degrees that he is ac-
cuftomed to more folid or fubftantial
diet.

Never fail to let an amufing fucceed a
ferious book, and to intermix poetry with
profe. Virgil is not lefs eloquent than
Cicero; his defcriptions, images, and
expreffions, give fancy and elocution to
thofe who poffefs it not naturally. Poetry
is the perfection of language; and if people do not apply to it while they are young,
they never acquire a tafte for it. It is impoffible, after a certain age, to read verfe
long, without having a real tafte for poetry.

Neverthelefs, moderate the ftudy of the
Poets; for, befides that they very often
take liberties contrary to good morals, it
is dangerous to grow too fond of them.
A young man who only fpeaks and raves
of verfe, is infupportable in company; he
is both a fool and a madman. I except
thofe whofe genius is only proper for effays
or exercifes of this kind; and then they
are recompenfed for this enthufiafm, by
the honour of becoming, like Danté, Ariofto,

ofto, Taffo, Metaftafio, Milton, Corneille,
or Racine.

Let the hiftory of the world, nations,
and countries be made familiar to your
children, without becoming a dry ftudy;
it fhould be accompanied with fhort and
accurate reflections, to teach them how to
confider events with judgement, and to acknowledge an Univerfal Agent, of whom
all mankind are but the inftruments, and
all revolutions the combined and fore-
known effects of his eternal Decrees.

Hiftory is only inanimate reading, if
they attend only to the dates and facts;
but it is a book full of life, if they obferve
the playing of the paffions, the fprings of
the foul, the movements of the heart, and
efpecially if they difcover a God, who,
always Mafter of events, produces, directs,
and determines them, according to his
good pleafure, and for the accomplifhment
of his fublime purpofes.

Our carnal eyes fee in this world only
a veil, which covers the actions of our
Creator; but the eyes of Faith fhow us,
that

310 LETTERS OF GANGANELLI,

that whatfoever happens is from one caufe, and that this caufe is truely God,

Take care that a good Rhetorician gives a tafte of true eloquence to your fons, rather by example than by precept. Make them comprehend, that **what is** really beautiful does not depend upon either modes or times ; and that if there are different ways of expreffing things according to different ages, there is only one of conceiving them properly.

Guard them againft **that** childifh eloquence, which, playing on words, is difgufting to true tafte ; and perfuade them that no gigantick ideas or expreffions ever enter into an elegant difcourfe. Altho' we ought never to be fated of true eloquence, man is fo fantaftical as to be glutted with it ; and it is owing to this, that we **fee** a fingular and trifling diction preferred to the commanding language of the Orators of the laft age. ·

There are men, and periods of time which have eftablifhed the ftandard of tafte in every thing; and it is on their productions that the eyes of your children

fhould

fhould be conftantly fixed, as the beft models; not, however, with flavifh ftrictnefs,
for they fhould not be fervile imitators of .
any perfon.

I love that the fancy fhould take wing,
and act from itfelf, inftead of being a copy
for want of invention. We have men of
fine parts; and we fhould have men of genius, if they did not too mechanically follow the beaten road. He knows little, who
knows only one path. The fpirit of invention is inexhauftible when we dare make
the attempt. I often tell my pupils, "Be
" yourfelves — think in your own way."
It is a melancholy thing to employ young
people, for whole years, in learning nothing but the **art** of repeating.

When your children have acquired the
age of maturity, then is the time to fpeak
to them, as a friend, of the nothingnefs of
the pleafures in which the world places its
happinefs; **of** the misfortunes in which
they engage us; the remorfe they excite;
the injury they do both to body and foul;
the abyfs they dig under our fteps, while
they appear only to fcatter flowers.

It

It will be no difficult matter for you to point out to them the dangerous rocks of fenfuality, either by vigorous expreſſions, or ſtriking examples; and to perſuade them that without idleneſs, the greater part of the pleaſures to which people addict themſelves ſo immoderately, would have no attractions. In idleneſs, as in ſleep, they form to themſelves the moſt brilliant ideas, and repreſent a thouſand agreeable chimeras which have no exiſtence.

When a ſon is perſuaded that a father talks only reaſon to him, and ſolely from tenderneſs, he hearkens to him, and his advice produces the beſt effects.

Laſtly, after having erected this edifice, there ſtill remains what I look upon as the moſt difficult of all—I mean, the choice of a profeſſion. This is commonly the touchſtone of fathers and mothers, and the moſt critical point for children.

If you will be perſuaded by me, you will give them a year to themſelves to reflect upon the kind of life that ſuits them, before you ſpeak to them of one profeſſion

fion in preference to another. The good
education they will have received, the
knowledge they will have acquired, will
naturally lead them to a happy iffue; and
there will be good reafon to hope they will
then decide for themfelves, according to
their inclinations, and according to reafon.

It will then be neceffary to fpeak frequently to them of the advantages and
difadvantages of the different conditions
of life, and to let them know how much
their temporal and eternal intereft is con-
cerned in the faithful difcharge of their
duty. The facerdotal and monkifh pro-
feffions furnifh ample matter upon the
ineftimable happinefs they muft tafte who
are truely called to them; and the terrible
calamities which they muft experience,
who have the rafhnefs to embrace them
without any but worldly views. The rank
of an Officer or a Magiftrate prefents a multitude of duties to difcharge; and it is fufficient to lay thefe duties before them, to
convince them of their importance.

After thefe precautions, and after having
often implored the affiftance of Heaven,

VOL. I.   P   your

your fons will enter refolutely upon the plan of life they have chofen; and you will have the confolation of being able to fay before God and man, that you have regarded their inclinations and their liberty. Nothing is fo fatal as for fathers to thwart the inclinations of their children; they expofe them to perpetual repining, and themfelves to the moft bitter reproaches, and even imprecations, which they have unfortunately deferved.

Since Providence has given you wealth, and you were born in a diftinguifhed rank, you fhould fupport your fons according to their fortune and condition; letting them however always feel fome wants, and keeping them always within the bounds of moderation, to teach them that this life is not the ftate of our happinefs, and that the higher they are raifed, the lefs ought they to become proud. Take care to give them money, that they may learn from yourfelf not to become mifers, and that they may have it in their power to affift the unfortunate. It will be proper to obferve with your own eyes the ufe they make of

it;

it; and if you find them addicted either to avarice or prodigality, you should lessen their allowance.

Lastly, my dear and respectable friend, attend more to the hearts than the under-standings of your sons: if the heart is good, all will go well.

Circumstances must teach you how to govern them; you should appear some-times indulgent, at other times severe, but always just and candid. Those young peo-ple who will not be wise, are distressed when they are reproved with a spirit of equity, because they find, against their inclination, that they cannot reply.

Leave them a liberal freedom, so that their father's house may not be their last choice; it is necessary that they should be happier there than elsewhere, and find those pleasures which may reasonably be expected from a parent, who though a friend to order, is indulgent from affection.

My pen hurries me on in spite of me :— as if it had sentiment, and relished the pleasure which I taste in speaking to you

you of your dear children, whom I love better than myfelf, and a little lefs than you. May God heap his bleffings upon them and they will be what they ought to be!—The education which you will give them muft bloffom to eternity. There it is that Parents reap the fruit of the good advice they have given to their children, and that worthy Fathers find themfelves, with their worthy Sons, to be for ever happy.

ROME, 16th Aug. 1753.

END OF VOL. I.

www.ingramcontent.com/pod-product-compliance
Lightning Source LLC
Chambersburg PA
CBHW060531030726
47498CB00004B/1157